Table of Contents

DEDICATION:

This book is dedicated to my family, without their support I would not be able to pursue my goals and live out my dream job: my wife, Michelle; my children, Carly, Alyssa and Riley; my parents, Bob and Nancy; my brother, Daniel; my in-laws, Mike and Sandra Kittrell; and my grandfather, Charles F. Skinner--whose love for the Clemson Tigers permeated everything he did; and finally to all of the Clemson fans--this one is for you.

Photos courtesy of Donny Knight and Zach Lentz

THE BUILD UP

Head coach Dabo Swinney stood on the putting green of The Reserve at Lake Keowee and displayed a smile that could not mean anything but football season is back in Clemson.

While the Tigers do not officially begin practice for two and a half weeks, for Swinney the annual media golf outing—followed by the trip to Charlotte for the ACC Kickoff— signals the start of football season, and it is something he is glad is finally here.

"Great to be out here. This is the official go time for us," Swinney said. "We started as a staff officially (Monday). Getting back going. There's a lot of enthusiasm in our building. Our players have worked hard this summer. That's one of the things I do when I do get away for a couple weeks. I try to keep a pulse of the team in various ways with what's going on and how they're working and this team has been very focused. And we've tried to give them some breaks along the way too. That's important.

"One of the things when they've come back from whatever break they've had, you could tell guys have continued to work. That is a sign of maturity and that's a sign of the veteran leadership and guys understanding what it takes and also being committed to what it takes. To be in a position to get off to a good start for fall camp. I think we're in a good spot there. But just anxious to get going."

It only took one question before Swinney was asked the question that is on the minds of every Clemson fan and media member since the spring game ended: Who will be the starting quarterback? But just as he did following the breakout performance by true freshmen Trevor Lawrence, Swinney stated that incumbent Kelly Bryant would enter the fall practice session as the No.1 quarterback—however the gap be- tween No. 1 and No. 2 is closing.

"I said after spring that I thought we had four guys that could compete to win this league with. Now we've got three because Hunter (Johnson) decided to move on. That hasn't changed, Swinney said. "How that's going to shake out? I know how we're going to start. Kelly (Bryant) is coming out of spring No. 1. He went into spring No. 1 and came out of spring No. 1. But the gap closed. We'll see what happens. It's a daily competition and a daily battle. I'm very confident in Kelly Bryant. I believe in Kelly. He can lead this team and has already proven he can do that.

"He's so much better today than he was this time last year. The same thing with Trevor and Chase. I know neither one of them have take a snap, but based on what I've seen in our practices and our meetings and who they are as people, those guys will have an opportunity to compete. I don't really have a timeline. It'd be great if all of a sudden (it was a) situation where you aren't even asking me the question. Then again, it's great to have a great competition too. I don't know if I really have had a situation where I could honestly say that we could compete with three guys. That's a good situation."

If Swinney's Tigers are going to make a run to the national title game for a third time in four years it will be because of the leadership of this years team—which enters as Swinney's most veteran team.

"Hopefully (it will help) a ton. It's well-documented that this is the most veteran team that I've had," Swinney said. "And I'm excited about that. Last year was the polar opposite. I embrace whatever challenge we have every year. I think that's fun. That's what makes college football so interesting.

Tigers picked to make a fourth straight playoff appearance

The Clemson Tigers football team has become used to being picked as a national title contender after three straight appearances in the College Football Playoff, twice as the No.1 team in the country and winning the national title in 2016.

But what makes the 2018 different than the three previous teams is that this team has experience, which means that the coaching staff can get after them a little more be- cause they understand what it takes to succeed.

"I think you can coach them hard right out of the gate, because they know. They know what it takes, they know what to expect," Clemson head coach Dabo Swinney said. "So, I think you can really, as a coach that's fun. Your starting point with a lot of these guys is in a different spot, but at the same time you've got other guys where you have to go right where they are and bring them along."

The Tigers return 62 letterman from the 2017 team, the most by six in Clemson history—including 17 starters, one shy of the school record of 18 set in 1977, 1981 and 1988.

It is the leadership of the veterans that has made the Clemson program, not one of the most dominant teams in the country, but one of the most consistent.

"One of the best things that's woven into the culture of our program, and one of the reasons that we've been so consistent, is the pride that our veterans take in nurturing the young guys and teaching them," Swinney said. "This is how we practice, teach- ing the position, teaching the concept, but also the core values of who we are. 'Nah, that ain't how we do things here.' So, that's a great position to be in as a coach too. It's like you've got a lot of guys helping to get that message the way it needs to be."

Maybe more important than having a group of players that telling the younger, more inexperienced players what to do is having a group of players that can explain why the Tigers do certain things the way they do them—

which is exactly what Swinney believes that he has in this year's team.

"Again, because you have to start over each year, to me anyway, and really rein- stall who, what, where, when, why," Swinney said. "And for a lot of these guys, these veteran guys, they know what to do. They know how to do it, but I think you take an- other step forward as a player when you really know why. When you really understand why it's important that you do your job this way, or this play, or this technique and how it impacts the overall call. I think we've got a lot of guys at that point, and we've got a lot of guys that are just learning what to do and that's all they can handle on their plate right now. Then they've got to figure how to do it, and then hopefully we'll get there someday."

While the expectations are as high as ever entering Swinney's 10 years as head coach, he is exercising cautious optimism over the fact that this team could be pretty good when the dust settles.

It's a good mix. I definitely think it's as deep of a team as we've had at the start- ing point," Swinney said. "We've got a lot of moving parts, but we've got the answers. So, I'm confident and I'm not concerned."

Putting Sugar Bowl loss behind them

If anyone around the nation is thinking that the Clemson Tigers are going to let their loss to Alabama in the College Football Playoff at the AllState Sugar Bowl last year beat them twice they are wrong.

In fact, the 2018 Tiger football team has put the disappointment of that New Year's Eve loss behind them and are ready for a new season.

"Nah, that's in the rearview mirror. We're just trying to beat Furman," head coach Dabo Swinney said. "That's really it. We move on from all that stuff and learn from it. That was disappointing at the time, but a lot of those guys on that team are not here anymore. A lot of them have moved on. It's a new team. New challenges and accept the challenge of a new season. New journey."

The reason that Swinney believes that the final game of last season will not beat the Tigers this season, is simple —the leadership and commitment that he has heard about during the offseason.

Coaches have not been able to be hands on with the players since the Orange and White game, but that has not stopped the players from hitting the practice fields on their own, and it is those reports that have Swinney believing this year will be a good one.

"I think there's going to be a ton of energy," Swinney said. "In fact, I was just talk- ing to Christian (Wilkins) driving up here and the guys are ready to go. They're chomp- ing at the bit to get started. We have a lot of veterans, but we've got as much competition as we've ever had. Everybody on this team, they know and they accept the fact

that they have to go earn it. Nobody's given anything and that's just the culture that

we have.

"That's the mindset - very much workmanlike. There's nobody that's arrived. Everybody has to go prove it. I don't care how many years that that they've started. Mitch Hyatt, he's a very proven left tackle, but this is August of 2018. He's got to prove it again."

The idea that nothing is given has been a staple of Swinney's program since he took over midway through the 2008 season. But it has been his commitment to that way of running his program that has gotten the most out of his players.

Whether a player is a five-star recruit like a Sammy Watkins or a walk-on named Hunter Renfrow—there is an excitement to see who put in the work during the offseason and is ready to go when their number is called in the fall.

"There's that mindset and we have so much competition at every position be- cause we do have good depth and have good experienced depth," Swinney said. "And everybody is working hard to earn the opportunity to play. Everybody can't start. But it's not about starting. It's about how you play when you play. That's where we are and with that comes a lot of energy and a lot of enthusiasm. It will be exciting to get out and watch them in camp."

CUinSanFran

The Clemson Tigers have one goal for the 2018 season and they made it known publicly on Twitter, Facebook and Instagram before the team turned off their social media accounts.

That goal was made clear with one hashtag— CUinSanFran.

The Tigers mission this year is to finish the season with a trip to the west coast to San Fransisco—or more specifically Santa Clara, California—site of the College Football Playoff National Championship.

"Absolutely. That's it," senior linebacker Kendall Joseph said. "That's where we're at, that's where Clemson's at, that's the goal. So, nothing short of that."

The Tigers opened this season at No.2 in the Coaches Poll, their highest preseason ranking since the 2016 season when the captured their second national title. The Tigers also open this season coming off a loss in the playoffs to the Alabama Crimson Tide—exactly like the 2016 season when they lost to the Crimson Tide in the 2015 championship game.

And just like they did in 2016, the Tigers are using that loss as motivation for this sea- son.

"We remember last year, but we are excited about this year," Joseph said. "We put the work in throughout the summer. We weren't sitting around moping, we just attacked it and it was one of the best summers I've been a part of."

One of the things that this team has that the 2016 team did not have is depth—as the 2018 Tigers returns 17 starters and 61 lettermen off of the 2017 team.

"We probably have a little more depth on this team than we did that year at certain critical positions," head coach Dabo Swinney said.

And it is that kind of leadership that Joseph believes will pay dividends when the season begins for the Tigers.

"It's awesome because there's so many voices of leadership," Joseph said. "It's not one guy just always talking or feeling like he has to talk. It's kind of just whoever feels moved to talk. Guys make sure that they let other people know that hey, you can speak up. I'm a senior linebacker and people might look to me to lead, but I look to J.D. Davis to talk or Judah Davis or Chad Smith or Jalen Williams. It's not just all about me because I'm the well-known old guy.

"I think that's what beautiful is having plenty of leadership throughout the team, so it's good."

However, all of the veteran leadership and the hashtags and the preseason rank- ings do not mean a thing when the ball is snapped Sept. 1—at that point it will be about how the Tigers take what they have done through the spring, summer and fall and put it to work.

"(Summer workouts are) just going to transition all throughout the year, and we'll see what happens this year," Joseph said.

THE QUARTERBACK BATTLE

Clemson head coach Dabo Swinney had enough of the questions about the battle be- tween senior Kelly Bryant and true freshman Trevor Lawrence—at least from the local media—as he implored those in attendance at his annual golf outing to give him a couple of weeks before being asked about the competition.

While those in the local media have begrudgingly obliged Swinney's request, the message did not make it to Charlotte—where the hottest topic at the annual ACC Kickoff was: who will be the Tigers' starting quarterback?

While Swinney would love to give an answer to the question, he admitted that the com- petition is good for all of the quarterbacks.

"It'd be great if I was in a situation where it was just y'all aren't even asking me the question (about the quarterbacks), but it's great to have great competition, too, because I don't know that I've really had a situation where I can honestly say that I think we can compete in our league with three guys," Swinney said. "Kelly is coming out of spring No. 1. He went into spring No. 1 and he came out of spring No. 1. But the gap closed, so we'll see what happens. It's a daily competition, a daily battle."

For Swinney the battle will ultimately be won by the quarterback who performs better in practice.

"We grade everything. (Quarterback's coach Brandon) Streeter does an unbelievable job. We have scrimmages. We have competitive work every single day. We do 7-on-7, team pass good on good. There is a lot that goes into the evaluation and it is not just the physical part of it," Swinney said to Tom Luginbill and Matt Schick of ESPN at the ACC Kickoff. "It's the mental part of it. There is so much evaluation mentally. Then it is how you respond - it's what's your demeanor, it's your coachability, what's your maturity, your ability to lead, how do you manage the game, how do you handle adversity. There is a lot that goes into that.

"But in college football, we don't have preseason games. So when we play it is for real. So sometimes you can decide things in camp. Sometimes it is close. If it is close then the next step is close. Then you might have a couple of guys play really well or someone will separate. That's where we are."

For Swinney and Streeter, one thing is very clear—the quarterbacks will be the ones who settle the battle on the field, in the classroom and during the Tigers' fall camp.

Because when they take to the field for the first time Aug. 3, the Tiger coaching staff will quickly learn who put in the time and the work required to lead the Tigers.

"They have to earn it first. If they earn playing time, then there are a lot of different ways you can play two quarterbacks or three quarterbacks," Streeter said. "I've seen it done before, so I think it is all about how you present it, how you prepare for it, but we have a couple of guys who have different parts of their game that they are better at than others.

"When you have a couple different kinds of quarterbacks it can be really stressful for the defense.

We will see how this thing pans out, but it is definitely something that we have talked about or considered, especially if they have earned it."

For Streeter, this is his first time having a quarterback battle that is drawing national attention. However, Swinney is an old hat at this, having to only look back four years to the start of the 2014 season—when true freshman Deshaun Watson was trying to unseat senior Cole Stoudt.

The one bit of solace that Swinney has had is that somebody has always separated him- self from the rest of the pack.

"You can't say, 'Well, we did this last year so this just carries over.' It does not work that way," Swinney said. "That is not the real world. It is not personal or anything like that. You give everybody the opportunity to compete and then you make dcisions as a coach based on what you have seen."

"If this guy is really good and this guy is good too, I don't think there is anything wrong with that. It really just has not been the case for us. We have not had that. We have always had somebody separate

Renfrow speaks out

When wide receiver Hunter Renfrow speaks, people listen—especially when the senior is talking about the Clemson Tigers' quarterback battle between true freshman Trevor Lawrence and incumbent Kelly Bryant.

However, unlike the media whose job is to find the conflict, he believes that it is his job to make sure that the battle does not rip the team apart.

"That is what a lot of people on the outside are going to try and do, to make a story out of it," Renfrow said. "We are just out there and we are a team. The best player is going to play. We are going to cheer for each other, no matter who runs out there. Whether it is Kelly or Trevor or Chase (Brice) or even (walk-on Ben) Batson. No matter who runs out there we are going to go out there and have fun playing football."

Even though the media around the country are looking to create a controversy surrounding the quarterback battle, Renfrow believes that the Tigers are in a great place because both Bryant and Lawrence are good enough to win with.

"They are both incredible," Renfrow said. "We were with them both during the spring and we were with both of them during the summer, so not much has changed. They both can sling it."

But even though both of the quarterback currently battling for the starting job an "sling it" there are some differences in the two players.

Bryant is the more mobile of the two quarterbacks, even though Lawrence displayed an incredible knack for evading and outrunning would-be tacklers this spring, and Lawrence has the stronger arm of the two.

With each quarterback bringing something unique to the position, Renfrow believes that he, like everyone else will have to wait to see who wins the job.

"Kelly can do things on the ground and is a very good manager. He can put the balls where he needs to, but so can Trevor. And Trevor has a lot of arm. We will see how it goes," Renfrow said. "We were watching highlights of Deshaun (today), and he had a great arm, but he put so much touch on it. All of the quarterbacks do different things well. Even if you have the best arm, it doesn't mean you throw the best ball.

Regardless of who wins the job, one thing is certain— there are no lifetime con- tracts at Clemson, which means everyone will have to make sure they bring their A- game every day.

"We have a lot of competition," Renfrow said. " aEvery single year it seems like everyone gets better so the competition is the same so you have to have that one rep mentality because you are going to get exposed out here.

"If I don't bring my best then K'Von Wallace is going to expose me. No matter who it is. The same thing that got us to the Sugar Bowl last year is going to get us back to the playoff this year, we just have to finish it this time. We are focused on winning the opener. If we take it like that then the rest will take care of itself."

Bryant won the battle

It was announced that the incumbent quarterback, senior Kelly Bryant, had won the hard-fought quarterback battle with true freshman Trevor Lawrence and redshirt freshman Chase Brice, and would start the Tigers' opening game of the season against the Furman Paladins Saturday.

While the announcement may have come as a surprise to many within the fan- base, who were waiting for Lawrence's name to be announced, it was Bryant all the way for the Tigers.

"I didn't really have a reaction. I was just like 'OK,'" Tiger defensive end Clelin Ferrell said. "He was the starter last year, so I didn't think I was supposed to be surprised. No matter who is back there, Chase, Trevor, Kelly, they can go back and win games. So I don't have too much reaction to it.

"In the spring, I feel like Kelly had the best spring out of all the quarterbacks. This summer I feel like Kelly played his best ball he's ever played. Trevor made a huge jump as well. Having to learn a whole new playbook as a freshman isn't easy."

While Bryant was the obvious choice for Ferrell, Bryant was relieved to finally get the word from Tiger head coach Dabo Swinney that he had won the job and would once again be charged with leading the Tiger offense.

"Coach Swinney brought me in and told me I would be running out there first. That was good to hear," Bryant said. "Being able to be the starter and run out there first with the guys, that is nothing new. I'm always going to prepare like I'm the starter, but now it is about performance.

"It is always good to hear from your coaches first hand. Like I said. I carry the same approach as if I am the starter and so now it is about performing each Saturday. Nothing is set in stone. This is just the first game so now I have to go out there and per- form."

Even though Bryant earned the starting job for the Tigers' opening game of the season against the Furman Paladins Saturday understands that he still must go out and prove himself every day in practice because there is a very talented true freshman lurking right behind him.

"I had to go prove myself right before camp. So now it is kind of the same thing," Bryant said. "I just focus on me. Of course, he is going to play. I know he is going to be ready. He is ready and he has shown what he can do. We have seen it in practice. Now, I just have to make sure I'm doing my job and just being great where my feet are and not worry about anything outside of that."

What set Bryant apart from the two challengers this fall was not his arm strength or his ability to evade would-be tacklers with his legs, instead it was his mental game.

It was his attitude that was a big area that he was challenged to improve between the spring game, in which he threw for an abysmal 35 yards, and the start of fall camp. It was those improvements, along with an emphasis on the passing game, that led to Bryant being named the starting quarterback for the 2018 season.

"I think for Kelly, it is his confidence right now is at an all-time high. He's managing all of the situations the way you want him to manage it, and then he's improved in the areas that we've asked him to improve--in terms of the throws that we've asked him to make down the field.

"I would say that his overall game management, his confidence, his leadership is the areas where he leads those guys."

3

DEFENSE WAS READY TO LEAD

Much of the talk around the ACC revolved around the Clemson defensive line that returned three All-Americans in Clelin Ferrell, Austin Bryant and Christian Wilkins and a projected top five pick in the 2019 NFL Draft in Dexter Lawrence.

That talk was in the form of questions about whether this is the best defensive line in the history of college football.—even to the point of asking the Tigers' All-American offensive lineman, Mitch Hyatt, about what makes that unit so special.

"Well, first off, they're just great guys," Hyatt said. "They're all-around just good guys, and I mean, the intensity they bring to practice and how hard they work is just -- they radiate it, and it comes off on everybody around them.

"When I am coming to practice, I know I'd better bring it because they're coming after me, so I need to match that intensity of theirs."

While his teammate was asked to sing the praises of the defensive line, Ferrell apparently had enough of the talk—resorting to plugging his ears in an effort to block out the distractions.

"You hit it right on the head. When I came in, Coach (Marion) Hobby, my old defensive line coach, and Coach (Todd) Bates, too, they always talked to us about not taking the cheese," Ferrell said. "Yesterday in the team meeting, Coach (Dabo) Swinney getting on us, "I hate seeing them old magazines. I hate that. It's all on paper."

"But they're right, though. I'm tired of seeing it, too."

While he, along with Swinney and his teammates, are tired of hearing and read- ing the hype surrounding the defensive line there is only one way to for the Tigers to end the talk—go out and play the game, which is exactly what they are ready for.

"We're ready to just go out there and play and perform because that's what it's all about," Ferrell said. "I mean, people just keep asking us how good can we really be? I mean, I don't know. We're very talented, but I hope I get asked this question at the end of the season. That would be a better time to answer it."

"(We're) not trying to listen to the outside noise because obviously I know we're a talented group. But we're more so about the action, we want to walk the walk rather than just talk it; know what I mean? "

Even being a part of, arguably, the greatest defensive line in the history of college football, Ferrell has an understanding that nothing is given—meaning each member of the Tiger defense had better make sure that they are ready to go every day.

"Our position rooms are very, very deep, know what I mean," Ferrell said. "And like Coach Swinney tells us all the time, you're not guaranteed to run out there first just because of what you did last year. You've got to go out there and earn it every single day, and that's something I love about it because that's how I got on the field.

"I had to go out there and compete with my peers in my position room when I was a redshirt freshman, to go out there and earn the starting job. So that's what you've got to do every day, so it's just going to bring the best out of all of us."

More than the front four

While the nation appears ready to see the Clemson Tiger defensive line in action for the first time this football season, the Tigers are ready to see something of their own—the young guns on the Tiger defense.

Included in that list of players are the nation's No. 2 ranked player, Xavier Thomas, the nation's No. 5 ranked player, K.J. Henry or any of the remaining seven players, all of whom are ranked at least a three-star— with four of them rated as four-star athletes.

However, one might think that the young Tigers may get lost in the shuffle with, arguably, the most talented defensive line in program history, but defensive lineman Clelin Ferrell has not seen any timidness with the newcomers—in fact, it has been the exact opposite.

"Oh, my goodness. Man, they've been great," Ferrell said. "I've always wondered like with just the hype that our defensive line gets, the front four, and then you still have guys like the No. 1 player coming in or a KJ Henry who's regarded as a five star. And people ask them why are you going to a school where they're already so-called deep in the defensive line.

"But it's because they know that they're not afraid to come in and compete. They understand the great tradition there, and they understand that they have guys that aren't just about themselves."

The unique thing about this very talented defense is that they have the combination of competitive drive and willingness to teach.

It is the leadership of the defensive starters, and a willingness to "only go 20 of 30 snaps as hard as they can, so they can save something for later in the season or in the fourth quarter," according to head coach Dabo Swinney, that makes this defense dangerous.

"We're all about each other. And I see those guys come in and be able to take constructive criticism and come in and work hard and make the progressions that they've made throughout the summer," Ferrell said. "Man, it's been huge, and I love that about them. I'm very hard on them because I want the best for them because if I see the best coming from them, it's only going to make me better.

"So it's been great to see them and they're making great progress, so I'm excited for the fall, their first fall camp coming up. It's like a dad seeing his kid go to school for the first time, know what I mean? Because they look up to me because they feel like I have some knowledge that is valuable to them. So I'm happy that I can be able to share some things with them, so it's been really, really good to see."

One thing is certain, the defense certainly has the talent to go down in Clemson, and national, history as the greatest defense of all-time, but first the seniors, juniors, sophomores and freshman must "walk the walk".

"(The defense is) not trying to listen to the outside noise because obviously I know we're a talented group," Ferrell said. "But we're more so about the action, we want to walk the walk rather than just talk it; know what I mean? "

Not Buying Magazines

If anyone was expecting Clemson defensive coordinator Brent Venables to be ex- cited about his defensive line being on the cover of Sports Illustrated, those people must not know Venables.

While Venables understands that it is not the players that choose to be on the cover of the magazine, but he is not about to run out to the store to buy a copy.

"If you said would you rather them be on it or not, I would say not," Venables said. "I'm not mad at them, it's not a big deal. Somebody actually just showed it to me right before I went into a meeting. I'm not frustrated by it at all. I'm just like, 'So?' I'm not like, 'Someone get me a copy and see if they'll sign it.' They're great guys, man. I'm not going to act like they don't deserve being praised.

"They're hard-working dudes, man. Humble, confident, good leaders, and give us everything we ask them. That being said, I'd rather all that stuff be done, but it's not their fault."

Even though Venables is not rushing out to get a copy of the magazine for his coffee table, the nation's highest-paid coordinator does see the value that type of exposure can have for the program as a whole—as long as the players remain grounded.

"I think it's good for our program, but you've got to keep it in perspective. I think they're a group of guys that can handle it. We coach them every bit as hard as we coach anybody on this team. And don't look the other way on anything. And don't cut 'em a break for anything. And they like it like that.

"If they were jerks, we'd quickly push them to the side or make an example of them. But for us, it's not hard to manage. They're very special."

If the Tigers are going to be a special group this season, they must first figure out the depth at the cornerback this season.

The Tigers lost cornerbacks Marcus Edmond and Ryan Carter to graduation, and safety Van Smith declared early for the NFL. Carter and Smith started last season, while Edmond's play was limited due to a foot injury.

The Tigers return only three cornerbacks with extended playing time — junior Trayvon Mullen, sophomore A.J. Terrell and senior Mark Fields — to go along with Brian Dawkins Jr. and former four-star cornerback LeAnthony Williams, who red- shirted last season.

However, the early returns on both true freshmen Mario Goodrich and Kyler McMichael have been exactly what they had hoped.

"I think both corners have had their moments where they've flashed and shown the ability to run and be physical and have some ball skills and awareness," Venables said. "Very natural tracking the football. Good instincts. Really, their knowledge and how they pick things up -- we do a lot -- and it's been good. They're handling the tempo of practice. We've got two pass skels up, so if you have two pass skels going on at the same time, then a lot of people are getting a lot of reps, and it's not easy to do. That's not something we've done forever.

"When you don't have great depth, everybody is doubling down on their reps, which is a good thing in regards to their development but can be really challenging to being in shape and whatnot. And it's not easy to do. We'll see how it goes when they're tackling. But they've done well, really, really well."

Even though the Tigers are in a better spot than they were in the spring, Venables is still not sold on the Tigers depth being great this season.

"If somebody pulled a hammy, all of a sudden you're back to issues," Venables said. "So we'll see as we start tackling and competing here in a couple weeks and see how guys are able to sustain we're they're at."

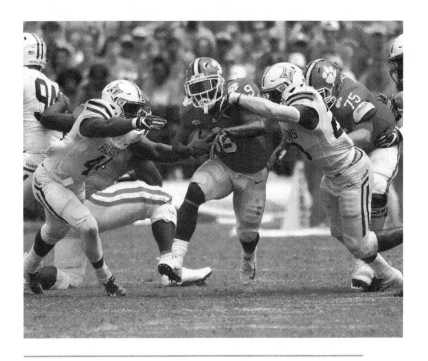

GAME 1: FURMAN

"The expectation is to come out and look like we've practiced," co-offensive coordinator Tony Elliott said. "To be a team that can compete on our practice field against one of the best defenses in the country, communication is of the utmost importance, drive the tempo...functioning in short-yardage situations and being able to dictate the game--that's the expectation.

"We're not worried about who's in front of us, we're worried about playing to the standard of Clemson and that's play fast, play physical, play hard and then go out and execute at a high level."

It was announced the person that will lead the 2018 Tiger offense onto the field this week's game would be senior quarterback Kelly Bryant—who won the job over true freshman Trevor Lawrence and redshirt freshman Chase Brice.

However, the depth chart that was announced for the opening game is good for just that—the opening game.

"The depth chart is just where you start, and it's going to change week-to-week and the guys know that every day they've got to come out to practice and compete," Elliott said. "There's competition at every position, obviously I know that there's one position in particular that's probably got the most focal point. But there's been great com- petition and you let the guys go practice, you put them in tough situations and them you evaluate how they do.

"Each coach has his own metric for how they evaluate their positions and it's tallied up daily. We have discussions about it and then we set the depth chart, let the guys go play and then we'll reevaluate it after the game to see if we need to make some changes."

While the fanbase is anxiously waiting to see Lawrence take the field for the Tigers, in his first game as a Tiger, Elliott is not worrying about when Lawrence will get into the game because his job is to prepare a game plan that will get the Tigers to 1-0 on the reason—regardless of who is calling the plays.

"That's a question for Coach Swinney, obviously him and Coach Streeter spent a lot of time talking about that and I don't know what the set plan is. I know that he said that both guys are going to play, and managing that is a delicate situation. So, I'm just excited to see that situation unfold when we get to the game. I know that he's said that Kelly is the starter and that Trevor has earned the right to play."

"The biggest thing is that we've got to get to the games and see how they perform in the game situation and then we'll take it week-by-week. We can't look ahead to Week 3, Week 4--we've got to focus on getting to 1-0 and beating Furman."

Not buying the lie

Don't tell the No. 2 Clemson Tigers that the Furman Paladins will be a "sure- fire" victory because the Paladins have had some success against the Tigers— albeit it was in 1936.

"People say this is a game we should win. Furman has beaten Clemson 10 times—10," head coach Dabo Swinney said. "So it's not like they've beaten Clemson once. The skies parted. I don't know when the last one was, but it has happened. Those ten times, Clemson was probably supposed to win. Supposed to doesn't get it done. You better show up every week. Openers are always tough. This will be tough for us."

Even though the Tigers were beaten in 1936, the Tigers' coaching staff is not go- ing to bring up the past when talking about this week.

In fact, they won't even dive into the recent past when discussing the success that the program has had—having never lost to an FCS foe since the creation of Division 1- AA (now FCS)—because around Clemson they talk about themselves and not the opponent.

"We have a standard and it doesn't change whether you're playing a 1-AA opponent or an opponent in the national championship," Swinney said. "That's how you develop consistency. How we play is based on how we prepare, effort, focus, attention to detail.

The Paladins return a very experienced team from last season, which saw them make a return to the FCS Playoffs.

It is that level of experience that make the Paladins a "stressful" team to prepare for.

"They have 10 of 11 starters back on defense who are juniors and seniors," Swinney said. "They're a veteran team with a lot of experience. All of their defensive linemen are back. They have a good group that knows what they're doing.

"Offensively, to be honest with you it's stressful to watch them. They do a great job. Shifts and motions, option offense, traditional spread looks, etc. They really stress you and do a great job with their play action game. They can expose you in a heart- beat. They threw the ball 20 times a game last year, but averaged 17 yards a catch. It's built off of their option principles. This will be a challenge. Each opener is tough be- cause you have not played. It's easy to see why they've had the success they've had."

Regardless of who the Tigers are playing Week1, this time of the year is a very special one for the players, coaches and the 100,000 fans that will descend on Clemson because it is finally game week.

"At the end of the day it's a special time," Swinney said. "The season starts now for a lot of people, especially our fans. For us, it started in January. It's off-season, it's mat drills, self-evaluation, spring practice, it's exit interviews, it's transformation, sum- mer grind, fall camp ... just a lot of boxes that are checked. But it all builds up to this moment. We have 12 opportunities that we're guaranteed. It's just exciting to know that it's finally here."

Quarterback Play:

Dabo Swinney addressed the quarterback competition Tuesday for the first time since the depth chart was released and he stated that the battle was the closest that he has had since he has been a head coach.

"Last year it wasn't close. It really wasn't. This year it's different," Swinney said. "Now, we have a proven guy, a guy who started 14 games and won a conference title. People get better and improve. I don't care where you start. Kelly Bryant has had a tremendous year of prep. I've had a front row seat. Bring a guy in here like Trevor Lawrence who is off the charts from a talent standpoint, but you don't know until you coach them. Trevor demonstrated this spring that he's one of these unique guys. He wasn't overwhelmed."

Even though Bryant won the starting job this week, Swinney made it clear that there are no lifetime contracts for the starting quarterback—especially when the battle is still very close.

"If something changes, we'll all see it. It's not like practice," Swinney said. "Y'all get to watch the games. Everyone will have a front row seat. Kelly doesn't have a 12- game contract. Trevor doesn't have a 12-game contract to continue to deserve to play. You're not entitled to play. It doesn't work that way. I don't have a lifetime contract. I have to prove that I should be the head coach. I have to earn that. That's life. These guys all understand that, man, let's go to work."

Another level to the Tigers

Clemson head coach Dabo Swinney thought when the final game was played last year it would be the last time that Christian Wilkins, Clelin Ferrell, Austin Bryant and Dexter Lawrence would play on the field together as Tigers.

But to his surprise, not one, not two, but all three of the draft eligible players re- turned to the Tigers for one final run at a second national championship.

"I really, to be honest with you, I thought of the three D linemen, Austin, Christian and Cle, I thought there was a good chance two came back, I thought one of them for sure," Swinney said. "I didn't think Christian would come back simply because he just graduated last December.

"Nothing surprises me with Christian. I think for him, he just loves college. If he would have gotten the grade, he probably would have gone. I think for him he knew he had an opportunity to continue to improve and finish a little better."

But for Swinney it was not only those three that were valuable.

There were numerous other players at other positions that had similar decisions to make, ultimately only three of the draft eligible players off the 2017 team chose to leave early.

"We had several guys. Kendall Joseph, Mitch Hyatt, Cle, Austin, certainly Christian. We had a lot of guys that I think were weighing a decision," Swinney said. "Those guys kind of got more pub, I guess. We just met and talked through it, then they kind of went about their process. I was just kind of waiting on letting me know."

And let him know they did—each in their own way.

Cle called me and told me that he was going to stay," Swinney said. "He kind of messed with me, called me on the phone, talked about how much he loved Clemson, how great it's been, appreciated everything, setting you up like he's getting ready to leave. Then he said, But that's why I'm going to stay another year.

"Anyway, it was kind of a fun moment there. They all kind of did it in their own way."

According to Swinney, one of the reasons the three defensive linemen chose to re- turn to school was to improve their draft stock—as none of the three graded out as a first-round selection. However, the danger for some players would be that they return only to focus on themselves and improving their draft positioning for the NFL Draft.

But even though Swinney addressed those issues with each player that decided to return, he was never concerned with the motives of the three linemen.

"All that stuff comes up in your conversation," Swinney said. "But, yeah, these guys, they're as big of team guys as I've ever been around. They're tremendous leaders. That's one of the reasons they came back, they were excited about working with the young guys. They didn't like how they finished last year, wanted an opportunity to be a part of an unbelievable legacy. These guys have won 40 games in three years.

"They're very in tune to the opportunity they have as a team. Certainly they want to do their part individually and better enhance their opportunities. These guys are team-focused all the way, no doubt about it."

The scary thing for opposing offenses in that Swinney believes there is another level to their play that they have not yet achieved.

"There's that in all of those guys. There is a level in Christian Wilkins, Kendall Joseph and Kelly Bryant you haven't seen," Swinney said. "The best is yet to come. There's a better version of Clemson or Coach Swinney you haven't seen. I don't want us to ever feel like we've arrived. Everyone has another level. You should get better as you go. (Dexter Lawrence) was awesome as a freshman and made all-conference last year but he wasn't 100-percent. He's just knowledge. He's experienced. Those guys came back to improve, with unfinished business."

The Game

80,048 orange-clad fans filled Clemson's Memorial Stadium Saturday to watch the No. 2 Clemson Tigers (1-0) take on the Furman Paladins (0-1), and the Tigers did not disappoint their fans, as they captured their 32nd straight victory over the Paladins by a final score of 48-7.

"It was just what we needed—we needed to play somebody. There is a lot to correct, but more than that we just needed to play somebody," head coach Dabo Swinney said."We accomplished our first goal—to win the opener.—but more than the we just needed to play somebody."

The Tigers opened the scoring on their second drive of the day, as Kelly Bryant (10 for 16 for 127 yards, one touchdown and no interceptions) found Amari Rodgers from 40 yards out to give the Tigers a 7-0. The touchdown was Bryants 15th career passing touchdown and the first career touchdown reception for Rodgers.

Following a three-and-out by the Paladins, Rodgers once again provided a spark for the offense, as he returned the punt 63 yards—which gave the Tigers the ball on the Paladin 20-yard line. The Tigers gained only two yards on the drive, as they settled for a 35-yard field goal from Greg Huegel and extended the lead to 10-0.

After a third punt of the day by the Paladins, the Tiger fans got what they had all been waiting for, as true freshman quarterback Trevor Lawrence (10 for 16 for 136

yards, three touchdowns and no interceptions) entered the game. The Tigers drove the ball to the Paladin 29-yard line before a sack on Lawrence meant the Tigers had to settle for a 49-yard field goal.

The Tigers took over at their own 5-yard line after a Furman punt, but the long field did not deter the Tiger offense.

On third-and-5 from the 10-yard line, Lawrence found Trevion Thompson for an 18-yard gain. Five plays later Lawrence showed how special he is, as he found Cornell Powell for a 42-yard gain to the Paladin 12-yard line. Three plays later he had his first career touchdown pass, as he found Deondre Overton from six yards out that ex- tended the lead to 20-0.

The Tigers got the ball back with 2:21 to play in the first half and quickly turned their last possession of the half into points, as Lawrence led the Tigers on a five-play, 38- yard drive that was capped off by an 8-yard touchdown run by Travis Etienne.

Bryant re-entered the game in the third quarter, and on the Tigers' second drive of the half led the Tigers' to the end zone. Bryant found Derion Kendrick for a 35-yard gain before he finished the drive on his own, as he scampered in from 35 yards and gave the Tigers a 34-0 lead.

Following another Furman punt, Lawrence once again led the Tigers to the end zone. The Tigers' went 93 yards in three plays—that included two rushes by true freshmanLyn-J Dixon for 77 yards and a Lawrence touchdown pass to Justyn Ross— and extended the lead to 41-0.

After a Furman fumble gave the Tigers the ball at the 12-yard line, the Tigers struck quickly, as Lawrence found true tight end Braden Galloway for the Tigers' final touchdown fo the game.

The Paladins finally broke through with 1:16 to play in the game, as Darren Grain- ger found Ryan DeLuca for a touchdown.

Tiger Tracks:

Tiger defense is stingy: The much talked about Clemson defense took the field for the first time in 2018 and did not disappoint. They held the Paladin offense to only 124 total yards of offense (94 rushing and 26 passing), while forcing two turnovers and allowing seven points.

Tiger offense balanced: The Tiger offense had as balanced a day as one could hope for, as they amassed 531 total yards of offense (277 passing and 254 rushing). Even more impressive than the yards amassed in the game was the fact that the Tigers did not commit a turnover on any of their 70 plays run.

Rodgers shines in punt return: Wide receiver Amari Rodgers talked all offseason about the work that he put in on returning punts—and it showed. The sophomore had two punt returns for 87 yards—including a 62-yard return that set up the first touch- down of the season.

Player Perspective: Albert Huggins on getting the first victory:

"We just went out there and dominated. We did exactly what we needed to do to- day—get that first win. Now, it's on to the next one."

Coach's Corner: Co-offensive coordinator Jeff Scott on whether the Tigers will continue to use two quarterbacks at Texas A&M:

"I didn't see anything on the sidelines that would eliminate those guys opportunities."

]

GAME 2: TEXAS A&M

Following the second-ranked Clemson Tigers' 48-7 victory over the Furman Paladins, one thing was immediately clear—the Trevor Lawrence hype-train has left the station.

And the true freshman did not disappoint, as the completed nine of 15 passes for 137 yards and three touchdowns—tying a the school-record for passing touchdowns by a freshman quarterback, set by former Tiger Deshaun Watson—a feat that was not lost on the coaching staff.

"You see what Trevor can do," head coach Dabo Swinney said. "He's a special talent, and he's just going to get better."

While Lawrence looked cool, calm and collected in the Tigers' opening game, in reality he was just like every other player on the field—nervous.

"I had a little bit of butterflies before I ran out there for my first series, but other than that wasn't too nervous," Lawrence said. 'Playing in the spring game kind of prepared me a little bit. Today was definitely more people."

The biggest challenge now will be living up to the expectations placed on him by the fanbase, and the media, following his first game as a Tiger. But for Lawrence, he is not concerning himself with the outside noise because it is a long season and this was just the first game.

"I don't really worry about that stuff (expectations). It's just nice to get this first one under my belt," he said. "I have a long season ahead, so I'm just trying to get ready for that. Trying to do that and do school and everything is just too much to put your- self if you worry about what other people are saying, so I'm not really worried about that stuff.

"I didn't really feel like I had anything to prove. We've been competing all spring and all fall. We've been handling everything on the field. I didn't feel like I had to prove anything, but I definitely wanted to have a good first game to start the season the right way."

Even after Lawrences' impressive debut, the Tiger coaching staff are sticking to their plan of playing multiple quarterbacks.

According to Swinney, neither quarterback did enough to separate from the other— meaning that when the Tigers' head to Texas A&M they will both have another opportunity to show that they deserve to be the starter.

"I didn't see anything that would say, 'This guy doesn't deserve to play.' Both had some mistakes, and both missed a couple of easy throws," Swinney said. "But I think that was just kind of the emotion and adrenaline of the first game. But they both settled in and made some big-time plays."

While the old adage says, 'If you play two quarterbacks, you don't have one,' Lawrence does not see it that way.

In fact, he believes that having the two quarterbacks rotating will only make the Tigers more dangerous because it only makes them better.

"It's been really good. It's definitely made me better, and I think it has made Kelly a lot better, too, with us competing," Lawrence said. "We have a good relationship, so it has been really good for us and the team. The coaches told me this week, and we had a plan, so I was ready for that. It worked out well. We've been doing that (rotating) in practice so we're used to it, and I'm used to it. It wasn't much different than practice."

Tigers familiar with Texas A&M

"It doesn't hurt. You still have to go out and play well and execute and it really matters what your players know," Venables said. "But there's some familiarity on both sides, so it can be negated to a certain degree. I'd rather have a little bit of background than not--for sure."

Even though Fisher is in his first season as the Aggies head coach, Venables believes that Fisher's current personnel fits just fine with what he wants to do—which is be very multiple and stress defenses in a lot of different ways.

"I think it fits very well. I mean, they've recruited extremely well--the skill, offensive line, quarterback, running back, receivers, tight end," Venables said. "I think there's a misconception that he's an I-back guy. He's going to run the I, he's going to run two-tight personnel, one-back, two-tight, two-back, he's going to line up with one- tight and two backs and he's going to line up in spread probably 60-65-percent of the time.

"That's who he's always been and that's what he's done. He knows how to utilize the personnel and put them in successful situations--in both scheme and situation-ally."

The Aggies opening game against Northwestern State, which they won by a final score of 59-7, saw a breakout performance by running back Trayveon Williams, who rushed for 240 yards and three touchdowns in only two quarters of play.

It is that kind of a back that has Venables concerned heading into Saturday's game.

"He's very explosive," Venables said. "Got great balance, good speed, instincts, can really accelerate--so he can run through trash, get outside and split the defense." While the Tigers will be making their third trip to College Station, the last coming in 2003, Venables is very familiar with the pageantry and with what to expect out of the the 102,000 fans, and he understands that the most important thing the Tigers must do to be successful is block out the noise.

"1996 was my first time at Kansas State and it's a very difficult place to play," Venables said. "Their fans are engaged from beginning to end, very well-prepared. There's a lot of pageantry with the military, and again their fans do a great job of stay- ing on cue. They put a lot of people in there, very passionate fanbase, prideful fanbase.

"We've been in a lot of tough environments and this will be another one. As much as anything, you've got to have poise to not get distracted because there's a lot going on outside of the field itself."

Swinney was ready for A&M

The No. 2 Clemson Tigers (1-0) traveled to College Station Saturday for a nationally televised game against the Texas A&M Aggies for the first time in 14 years.

But even though both teams have already played and won their opening game, for the Clemson Tigers, this felt like a second opening game.

"We have a big challenge this week for sure. A huge challenge," head coach Dabo Swinney said. "It's like another opener. We don't know a lot about Texas A&M. The unknown is a competitive advantage for them. Hopefully our experience can be an advantage for us.

It's a difficult game for us to prepare for. We don't have a lot of video evidence on them."

Defensively, the Aggies are led by former Notre Dame and Wake Forest defensive coordinator Mike Elko— who inherited a very talented defense that allowed 406 yards of offense last season.

"Defensively they are stout. They've got some big dudes up front. (Daylon Mack) is an earth-mover. (Landis Durham) led the SEC in sacks last year. Very talented. They have a lot of guys on defense who started last year," Swinney said. "Their d- coordinator came from Notre Dame and he was at Wake Forest. I was really, really happy when he left and went to Notre Dame because he was one of the best that we saw year in and year out.

'He does a great job schematically, especially coaching those guys up in the secondary. I think they do as good a job as anybody at route reading and diagnosing the play. It should be a challenge to figure out what their plan is going to be and making the right adjustments to give our guys a chance to be successful."

The Aggie offense got the boost they were looking for out of new head coach Jimbo Fisher, as they put up 758 yards of offense in their Week 1 victory over Northwestern State.

For Swinney, it was not the amount of yards the Aggies gained that was impressive—it was the way in which they gained those yards, with 503 yards coming on the ground.

"Offensively, very impressed with their quarterback. The more I watched of him, really impressive athlete," Swinney said. "He actually came to camp one summer. He's incredibly athletic and he's got a lot of moxie. He won me over when I watched him run the read option and he pitches the ball and then he's 20 yards down the field lead- ing the way blocking. He's gritty. It's very easy to see how he's won his team and has become a leader for them. Made some big-time throws.

"(Jace Sternberger) transferred in there and he fits the mold of what Jimbo has always had in the past at tight end. They rushed for 500 yards. I know the team didn't match up with them well but it's hard to rush for 500 yards, I don't care who you play."

While this will be the first trip in 14 years for the Tigers to Kyle Field and Texas A&M, Swinney remembers vividly the trip that he made with the Tigers, as an assistant coach, and the 27-6 beatdown that ensued.

"I was a part of that butt whipping we took in 2004. We couldn't get home soon enough. We got destroyed out there. I remember all too well," Swinney said. "That's the only time I've ever been in Texas for a football game as a player or coach. I remember that was my second year here and we flew out there. It seemed like we stayed an hour and a half away. We were a long way away. Back in those days we wore our warmups. We got on the bus and there was no air conditioning.

"I remember vividly getting off the bus and everybody had their pants pulled up and their shirts off. We looked like North Dallas 40 getting off the bus. We were a bad looking bunch and everybody was sweating. In my mind, I remember going, 'This is fix- ing to be a long day,' and it was. They absolutely kicked our tails all over the field that night."

Regardless of whether or not the Tigers emerge from Saturday's game with a victory or not, one thing is certain—these are the kind of games that make teams better.

"This is a complete team that we're getting ready to play," Swinney said. "We have a lot of respect for Jimbo Fisher. He'll have his guys ready with a new energy and new chemistry. I want to see our team go on the road and stay focused and display our experience and adjust to the adversity within the game.

"This is the type of game that makes you better. It gives you a chance to grow your team as you get through the season."

The Game

The second-ranked Clemson Tigers (2-0) traveled out west Saturday night and, in front of 104,794 fans, defeated the Texas A&M Aggies by a final score of 28-26—and secured their first victory in the state of Texas since the 1939 Bluebonnet Bowl.

"In the end, we found a way to win by two points. We're 2-0 and that's what awe came out here to do," head coach Dabo Swinney said. "Just really proud of our team— what dogfight—and it is a shame that somebody has to lose."

On the biggest of stages, it appeared that the Tigers also found their quarter- back—as, after trading series' with true freshman Trevor Lawrence, Kelly Bryant led the Tiger offense with 258 yards of total offense (205 passing on 12-of-17 with one touchdown, and 53 rushing yards and a touchdown).

"He was just locked in the whole game," Swinney said. "I thought he made some really big-time throws, runs and did exactly what we know he can do...There's no doubt that Kelly settled in the fourth quarter and gave us exactly what we needed to get a win."

The Aggies opened the scoring in the first quarter, after an eight-play, 32-yard drive ended with a Daniel LaCamera field goal that gave the Aggies a 3-0 lead.

The Tigers responded on their next drive, as Bryant led the Tigers on a seven- play, 75-yard touchdown drive— highlighted by an Amari Rodgers 64-yard reception on third-and-15 and a Bryant touchdown run.

Following an Aggie punt, Lawrence entered the game for the Tigers and needed only one play to go 64 yards for the Tigers' second touchdown of the game, as he found Tee Higgins for the touchdown that put the Tigers ahead 14-3.

After the Tigers went three-and-out on their opening drive of the second half, the Aggies quickly cut into the lead—as they drove to the Tiger 23-yard line and settled for a 40-yard field goal that cut the Tiger lead to 14-6.

After Lawrence opened the second half, Bryant entered the game on the Tigers' third series and quickly found Higgins for a 50-yard gain on first down. It took the Tigers only three additional plays before the Tigers' found the end zone, as Bryant found Overton and put the Tigers ahead 21-6.

The Aggies needed only two plays go 78 yards for their first touchdown of the game, as Kellan Mond found Camron Buckley for a 69 yard gain before he found

Kendrick Rogers for a 9-yard touchdown pass that cut the lead to 21-13.

Bryant and the Tigers responded in a big way on their ensuing possession, as Bryant found Hunter Renfrow for a 40-yard gain on first down and again found Renfrow for a 10-yard gain that gave the Tigers the ball at the Aggie 8-yard line. The Tigers needed only two plays before Travis Etienne finished off the drive with a 1-yard touchdown run.

However, Mond and the Aggies responded on their next drive—aided by two 15- yard penalties—Mond led the Aggies on a six-play, 75-yard touchdown drive, capped off by a 14-yard reception by Quartney Davis that cut the lead to 28-20.

The Aggies got the ball back with 1:12 to play in the game, but needed only 26 seconds to find the end zone to cut the lead to 28-26. However, the 2-point conversion attempt was intercepted in the end zone by Mark Fields and secured the Tiger victory.

Tiger Tracks:

Gameday winners: With their victory Saturday night, the Tigers have now won nine of their last 10 contests in which they were featured on ESPN's College Game- Day —including each of their last six since 2016.

Bryant in the top 10: With his pass completion to Amari Rodgers in the third quarter, Kelly Bryant moved into the the top 10 in school history in career completions— passing quarterbacks coach Brandon Streeter.

Tigers' air it out: The Tigers hit on a pair of 64-yard passes in the first half of play, as Bryant found Rodgers and Lawrence found Higgins—both passes led to to touchdowns for the Tigers. It was the first time in school-history that the Tigers have had two passes of 60-plus yards in one half by two different quarterbacks.

Power Rangers do it all: Known for their dominant defense line play, the Power Rangers made their presence felt in the special teams department, as Dexter Lawrence, aided by Christian Wilkins, blocked a 49-yard field goal attempt in the second quarter to preserve the Tigers' 11-point lead.

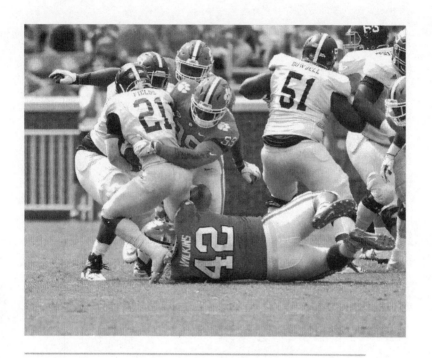

GAME 3: GEORGIA SOUTHERN

When the lights were the brightest and the second-ranked Clemson Tigers needed to find a spark they did not turn to their upstart true freshman Trevor Lawrence.

Instead the coaching staff went with the senior Kelly Bryant, whose moxie and poise helped lead the Tigers to a 28-26 victory over the Texas A&M Aggies.

"I thought he really kind of settled in and played well," head coach Dabo Swinney said. "He made some really big-time throws, huge runs, he took care of the ball, man- aged the game and that's what we needed him to do in some really critical situations-- that's what we needed him to do. In some critical situations he showed a lot of poise. It was good to see.

"There is no doubt that I thought that Kelly, in the fourth quarter, really settled in and gave us the experience that we needed in that moment to get out of here with a win."

Bryant, who led the Tigers in total offense with 259 yards of offense, has been known for what he can do with his legs. But, when the Tigers needed him the most Saturday night, he proved he could be a weapon throwing the ball.

With the entire nation watching, Bryant threw completed 12 passes for 205 yards— with a career-best passing efficiency of 191.3. Bryant also moved himself further into the Clemson record books, as he passed Steve Fuller and quarterbacks coach Brandon Streeter, moving into the top 10 career completions.

But for the team-first Bryant, the focus was on his team.

"We learned a lot. Coming into an environment like this and we got our backs against the wall, not really playing good, not complementing the defense and special teams and we just find a way to win," Bryant said. "There was a lot of unknowns about A&M, we didn't have a lot on film about that team from this year. But we're battle tested and we just find a way to win.

"On the road, late game early in the season, a lot fo unknowns about this team but you know it was good. To get that under our belt, you know, learn from it. You know it wasn't always pretty, but we just kept battling. You know that just says a lot for this team, just finding ways to win—you know, when it's not pretty."

After a shaky start to the game, Bryant settled down, that included a fumbled snap on the 1-yard line, and hit his stride in the second half of the game—when the Tigers needed him the most.

"Just settling in, just getting in a rhythm was really the biggest thing. We weren't really in a rhythm early on," Bryant said. "So, just getting in rhythm, taking it one play at time and just playing fast and executing."

While many around the country will look at how close the game was—a two- point victory—and wonder what went wrong for the Tigers, Bryant believes that he learned a lot about himself and his teammates Saturday night.

"One thing I've got to learn from it to stay poised and just settle in," Bryant said. "That's something I've said a lot, but when you actually go through an experience like that it tells you a lot about yourself."

"Just mentally that we was locked in. Just not letting anything get to me, just staying poised and just keep playing and just try and be that leader. Whenever I'm not in the game get on the sideline and talk to my guys, be encouraging and make the plays when it's there. Just do my job, and that's the thing I've been doing the whole year."

Even though Bryant was the better quarterback Saturday night, Swinney made it clear that Lawrence will still play this season saying, "You have seen what a special talent he is...We are going to need him."

For many players, hearing their head coach say that would be disheartening and may cause them to lose the focus and the edge necessary to play at the level of the Clemson Tigers, but that is not who Bryant is.

And he is not going to use the decisions of the coaching staff as a reason for excuses.

"I'm not going to use that as an excuse," Bryant said. "That's early on when I was in missing plays and the only thing I was doing was just staying engaged on the sideline--making sure that I am being encouraging. You know, Trevor came in and straight out of the gate made a big play--got the offense a spark. So, I just made sure that I was engaged and all. I didn't feel like that was the reason that I wasn't in rhythm.

"The biggest thing was to try and not make it more than what it was. We got the experience on both sides of the ball that we can lean on--that's what we did tonight."

Swinney remembers 9/11

9/11 is a day that lives emblazoned in the hearts and minds of every American.

They can tell you where they were, what they were doing, who they were with and even what they were thinking the moment the planes began to hit the World Trade Center, a field in Pennsylvania and the Pentagon.

The same holds true for Clemson head coach Dabo Swinney, who was on his way to work at AIG Baker, having been out of coaching in 2001.

"It was about an hour and 15 or 20-minute drive every day from Tuscaloosa to 280. I was on 459 and I was listening to one of the radio stations talking football," Swinney said. "I used to use that time as prayer time and quiet time and I'd catch up with what was going on in the sports world. I was my first time not coaching so

I was thinking about what I had to do that day at work or whatever. I'll never forget it.

"I was telling Kath (Kathleen Swinney) last night that I couldn't believe it was 17 years ago. I was driving down 459 in my green Tundra. I was driving down the road and they came over and interrupted the radio and just started talking about that there had been a plane crash but they didn't know what was going on. Then all of a sudden, everything gets consumed on the radio I'm listening to and in my mind, I'm going, 'Man, this can't be real.' It was a very surreal moment. I listened on the way and then I got to the office and it was a very emotional day."

Swinney echoed what every American felt that day—fear. Fear for the day. Fear for the days to come and fear for what the future would mean for his two boys.

"It was an incredibly emotional day for everyone. It was a scary day," Swinney said. "As a company, there was nothing done that day. We sat and we watched TV and we listened and nobody could believe what we were seeing. It was just heartbreaking and gut-wrenching and incredibly emotional. I just remember thinking about my three year old and my two year old and the world that they're going to grow up in. It was unbelievable. It impacted so many things in this country."

Two years ago, the Tigers made their biannual trek to Boston College for a foot- ball game against the Eagles, but this was not an ordinary football game—it was the Red Bandanna Game.

The game honors former lacrosse player Welles Crowther, who is remembered for his acts of heroism and bravery during the Sept. 11 terrorist attacks.

Crowther lost his life but not before he led at least a dozen people to safety in the South Tower of the World Trade Center complex. Crowther had opportunities to save himself but chose to return to the towers in hopes of leading more people to safety.

He became known as "The Man in the Red Bandanna" and during this one foot- ball game, fans wear red bandannas while the players and coaches wear specially de- signed apparel designed especially for the game.

For the Tigers head coach there is something special about being a participant in the game.

"I know there are a lot of people out there today whose lives were saved because of the sacrifice of others. I think about the kid with the red bandana," Swinney said. "I think about his parents. In fact, I've still got the red bandana and carry it my briefcase. It stays in my briefcase. I think about his mom and dad and how this kid saved others people's lives. You never know how you might respond in a situation like that, but an incredibly difficult day for our country. I wasn't alive during Pearl Harbor, but I can imagine it was probably a similar feeling for this country."

While most of his players were mere babes when the attacks occurred, Swinney will take time today to educate his player on what that day meant to America because it is a day that no one should ever forget.

"I think it's great to take some time today and pause and reflect on all of the people who lost their lives, the impact that it had on all of their families, the children who lost moms and dads," Swinney said. "Then all of the unbelievable brave and heroic people that I saw that day. The old saying, there's a difference between running away from a fire and running to it, and people who were running through it and to it, it was amazing heroism from so many people. The policemen, the firemen, the first responders that lost their lives trying to save others.

"Hopefully, it's not something we ever have to deal with again. It was a tough day and one I'll never forget."

Bryant always had confidence

For Clemson quarterback Kelly Bryant, there have always been those who said he would never be able to have success as the leader of the Tiger offense.

Even after leading the Tigers to a 12-2 season, a third straight ACC title and a third straight appearance in the College Football Playoff, Bryant still faced the same questions that he had faced prior to last season—in part, due to the arrival of true freshman Trevor Lawrence.

But even when the rest of the world was seemingly against him, his belief in him- self never wavered.

"I already had that confidence in myself," Bryant said. "There was always questions brought up to me about my game, can't do this, can't do that. But I just stayed the course, just continued to grind and just do my job being a leader on this offense and just continue to work. That's pretty much been my story and the story for this offense. Just always being questioned, just being doubted, but finding a way to get the job done."

Even though Bryant exited the spring and entered the fall as the Tigers' starting quarterback, he understood that if he was going to hold onto the job he would have to improve in certain areas, namely, he needed to get better throwing the ball and not just relying on his legs to get him out of trouble—which he did.

"I feel like my trust in the pocket has grown. It just comes with experience and having those game reps that I've had and that experience that we were talking about," Bryant said. "It just makes me more comfortable, just trusting my reads a little bit longer and also having that time clock in my head where I can't hold the ball too long and just get ready to throw it away or make a play with my legs as well."

Bryant's work this offseason paid off, as the Tiger offense have amassed six plays of 20 yards or more this season—after finishing with only 11 such plays all of last sea- son— which ranks No. 1 nationally.

"We want to be more of an explosive offense. Get the explosive plays back," Bryant said. "And I feel like we did that last week. It opened up the whole offense. We can make plays down field and soften the coverage up where we can run the ball, just give defenses something they have to look for, not just stacking the box and forcing us to make plays. Now they have to worry about the run and the pass."

However, part of those explosive plays have come at the hand of Lawrence—who entered last week's game and threw a 64-yard touchdown pass on his first play from scrimmage.

While Bryant is still splitting snaps with the true freshman, he understands the importance of keeping his focus—even when he is not in the game.

"When coach told me he was going in, I knew what the situation was," Bryant said. "He told me just make sure I'm engaged and make sure I'm getting the play calls as well and make sure I stay ready because you never know depending on the situation I was going to get thrown back in. Also that's the same thing he's been telling Trevor as well. So that's what we've been doing is a good job of making sure we're locked in and just focused and make sure we're ready when the opportunity presents itself."

Bryant's belief and trust in himself, combined with his growth learning his craft, has been something that head coach Dabo Swinney has been impressed with—especially in the Tigers' 28-26 victory at Texas A&M.

"I thought his leadership and his toughness down the stretch were awesome. It was what we needed in that moment," Swinney said. "Kelly did a good job of playing well, being confident, focused and composed. He has been a true example of staying focused."

The Game

The threat of Hurricane Florence did not stop the 79,000-plus fans who traveled to Clemson to watch the second-ranked Tigers (3-0) take on the Georgia Southern Eagles (2-1) Saturday.

As the storms closed in on small town, the Tigers emerged with a 31-7 victory over the Eagles—however, the Tigers appeared a little sleepy for the noon kickoff.

After not committing a turnover in their first two games, the Tigers committed two turnovers in the opening quarter of play. An interception on the Tigers' opening drive and then a fumble by Adam Choice on their third drive of the game bookended a missed 40-yard field goal by Greg Huegel.

After the slow start, the Tigers turned to true freshman Trevor Lawrence, who finished the game with 194 yards passing, one touchdown and one interception).

On his second drive of the game, Lawrence led the Tigers on a 13-play, 93-yard drive that featured passes of 17 yards to Milan Richard and a 31-yard reception by

Hunter Renfrow before Travis Etienne finished off the drive with a 1-yard touchdown run.

After another punt by the Eagles, Bryant re-entered the game, but was removed after suffering an injury. But that did not stop the Tigers, as Lawrence needed only one-play before he found Justyn Ross for a 57-yard touchdown that gave the Tigers a 14-0 lead.

Following a 43-yard punt by the Eagles, the Tigers and Bryant went back to work on the ground, as Etienne amassed 66 of the Tigers' 76 yards on the drive. Tavien Feaster capped off the drive with a 1-yard touchdown run and gave the Tigers a 21-0 lead at the half.

After the Tiger touchdown, Bryant was taken to the locker room—where he remained until 1:45 to play in the third quarter.

The Tigers continued to add to their lead following the Eagles sixth punt of the game. Lawrence led the Tigers to the Eagles 9-yard line before an unsportsmanlike conduct penalty forced the Tigers to settle for a 37-yard field goal by Greg Huegel.

After Huegel's second missed kick of the day, the Eagles broke the shutout. After a trick-play gained 40 yards, quarterback Shai Werts scampered in from six yards out and cut the lead to 24-7.

The Tigers extended their lead back to 24 points, after Etienne rushed two times for 46 yards, including a 40-

yard touchdown run that capped a two-play drive. On that touchdown run, Etienne surpassed the 1,000-yard mark for his career.

The Tigers added a final score, this time on a 10-yard run by Adam Choice that capped a six-play, 73-yard drive that extended the lead to 38-7.

Tiger Tracks:

Travis Etienne's 118 first-half yards gave the sophomore his second-career 100- yard game.

The Clemson Tigers had their third scoring drive of 90 yards or more already this season. Clemson had four scoring drives of 90 or more yards in 14 games in 2017.

On the sixth play of the Tigers' opening drive, Mitch Hyatt played his 3,000th career snap and became only the fifth player in Clemson history to play 3,000 career snaps from scrimmage

GAME 4: GEORGIA TECH

The No. 2 Clemson Tigers have had their ups and downs on their way to a 3-0 start to the season. But one thing that is way up is the Tigers' explosive plays.

The Tigers finished the year with 11 plays of 40-plus yards, and have already nearly matched their total with nine plays of 40 or more yards this season—which ranks the Tigers second in the nation behind only Memphis (11).

"I thought at times our tempo was better really on some of those drives we were running the ball, able to repeat some plays," co-offensive coordinator Jeff Scott said. "That's our third week in the row with some good explosive plays. I believe we had 10 explosive plays, runs over 12 (yards) or passes over 16 (yards) so that was a positive, that's been a big emphasis obviously from last week."

A large part of the Tigers' resurgence in the explosive play department has been as a result of a commitment to the run with Travis Etienne, the arm of true freshman Trevor Lawrence and the play-making ability of wide receiver Justyn Ross.

"There were lots of positives, offensively. Eighteen different guys touched ball for us," head coach Dabo Swinney said. "Travis Etienne played well; he had a career-high 162 rushing yards. All of our running backs did good things. We ran the ball like we needed to. After Kelly Bryant went out with a chest bruise, Trevor Lawrence did a lot of good things, too. He made some big throws, but he missed some throws, too, [ones] that he probably wishes he could have back. Also, Justyn Ross showed everyone that he's a really special player by getting 103 receiving yards. Again, overall, there were lots of positives on offense."

However, if the Tigers are going to make a run at a fourth straight ACC Champi- onship and a fourth straight appearance in the College Football Playoff they will need to capitalize on all of their opportunities— which they did not do in Saturday's 38-7 vic- tory over Georgia Southern.

The Tigers turned the ball over three times, two interceptions and a fumble, while missing two field goals of 38 and 47 yards—leaving a bad taste in Swinney's mouth.

"I was a little frustrated it took four plays to get in the end zone. I just wasn't really happy. So I put the other guys in," Swinney said. "And they responded. Sometimes you gotta get people's attention and make sure they're hungry. When you're hungry, you don't leave chicken on bone, and we left too much chicken on the bone to- day."

The idea of there being too much food left on the plate was echoed by co- offensive coordinator Tony Elliott— who believes that the Tigers were too inconsistent.

"We wanted to come out and run the football and establish the run," Elliott said. "Overall, [I] just loved the effort. I thought we were ready to play [but] we just have to be more consistent. We had a couple drives where we shot ourselves in the foot with penalties and weren't able to capitalize."

But regardless of how much food was left on the plate, the Tigers have found the big-play while playing numerous players in each of their first three games— which will only make them more dangerous as the season progresses.

"Eighteen different guys touched ball for us. Travis played well. All of our running backs did go," Swinney said. "Man that's Clemson football at it's best. A lot of guys getting the opportunity to grow and develop."

The Game

A sea of orange invaded Atlanta and watched the second-ranked Clemson Tigers (4-0, 1-0 ACC) put together their best performance of the season Saturday, as they dominated the Georgia Tech Yellow Jackets (1-3, 0-2 ACC) by a final score of 49-21 at Bobby Dodd Stadium.

"I'm really proud of our team, I thought this was our best game of the four games to this point," head coach Dabo Swinney said. "Our ability to stop the run and to run the football has been critical to us having success in this game...I'm just really proud of our team.

"Our fans gave us a great environment to play in. We will enjoy this one tonight. I think we took a step forward as a football team today."

With the victory the Tigers moved to 4-0 on the season for the fourth straight sea- son, won their opening ACC game for the fourth straight season and defeated the Yellow Jackets for the fourth straight season.

After both teams exchanged punts on their opening drives, the Tigers found the end zone on the Yellow Jackets' second possession of the game.

On third-and-20 from their own 19-yard line, Yellow Jacket running back Que Searcy rushed for a 15-yard loss before Tiger linebacker Tre Lamar caused a fumble that was recovered by defensive end Clelin Ferrell in the end zone for a touchdown.

"Really pleased with how we played defensively, and to see them score was incredible," Swinney said.

After a Georgia Tech missed 33-yard field goal gave the Tigers turned to true freshman Trevor Lawrence (13-16 for 176 yards, four touchdowns and no interceptions), who entered the game for starting quarterback Kelly Bryant, to provide a spark to the offense that had been stagnant.

And Lawrence did not disappoint, as he led the Tigers on a seven-play, 74-yard drive that was capped by a 19-yard touchdown pass to Hunter Renfrow that gave the Tigers a 14-0 lead.

After a Yellow Jacket punt, the Tigers wasted no time adding to their lead. After a 2-yard rush by Adam Choice moved the ball to the Clemson 47-yard line, Lawrence showed off his arm—as he found Justyn Ross for a 53-yard touchdown.

"I keep telling the guys, 'We need to throw it to this guy a little more," Swinney said. "It seems like every time he touches the ball he scores."

The Tigers got the ball back after the Yellow Jackets third three-and-out of the first half, but gave the ball right back to the Yellow Jacket—as Lawrence was intercepted by Desmond Branch after the ball hit offensive lineman Gage Cervenka in the head.

Tech needed only four plays to cut the Tigers' lead to 14 points, as quarterback TaQuon Marshall scrambled into the end zone from 11 yards out.

However, Lawrence and the Tigers responded on their next possession. Starting at their own 36-yard line, Lawrence orchestrated a 12-play, 64-yard drive that ended with Lawrence finding Travis Etienne for 3-yard touchdown that gave the Tigers a 28- 7 lead at the half.

The Tigers decided to attack the Yellow Jackets on the ground to open the second half, as the combination of Etienne and Tavien Feaster combined for 74 yards on a drive that featured a 27-yard touchdown run for Feaster.

After a punt of 48 yards by the Yellow Jackets, Bryant returned for the Tigers and led them to the end zone for the second time in the third quarter and extend the lead to 42-7.

The Yellow Jackets continued to fight. After a 75-yard touchdown drive that was aided by two personal foul penalties on the Tigers, the Yellow Jackets punched the ball into the end zone and cut the Tigers' lead to 42-14.

The Tigers used their third quarterback of the day in the fourth quarter, as Chase Brice entered the game. However, on Brice's first drive, his second pass of the day was intercepted by Yellow Jacket defender Malik Rivera—who returned the interception 42 yards to the Tiger 33-yard line.

The Yellow Jackets added their final score of the game, as quarterback TaQuon Marshall found Clinton Lynch from 5 yards out to cut the lead to 42-21.

The Tigers wanted to keep the pedal down, as Lawrence returned to the game and led the Tigers on a 5-play, 77-yard drive that took only 2:13, and was finished off by

Lawrences fourth touchdown pass of the day—a 30-yard strike to Tee Higgins.

Tiger Tracks:

Trevor Lawrence's touchdown pass to Justyn Ross was the second time in the last two weeks the two have connected for touchdowns of more than 50 yards.

Clemson placekicker Greg Huegel (295) passed James Davis (294) for sixth-most career points in school history.

Clelin Ferrell's touchdown on the fumble recovery in the first quarter was the first by a Clemson defensive lineman since Carlos Watkins scored against Appalachian State in 2015.

Tavien Feaster just broke 1,000 career yards on that TD run. That marks the second straight week a Tiger back has reached the end zone on a run that pushed them over 1,000 career years after Travis Etienne accomplished the feat last week.

Clemson linebacker Chad Smith was ejected in the third quarter for targeting and will miss the first half of the next game.

Player's Perspective:

Quarterback Trevor Lawrence playing in front of his hometown crowd and throw- ing four touchdown passes.

"It was really cool to be able to come out and play that way. I had a lot of people here today, but our fans travel really good all the time."

THE CHANGE

Through the first three games of the 2018 season, the coaching staff for the second- ranked Clemson Tigers remained very consistent with regards to who had the lead in the quarterback battle between incumbent Kelly Bryant and true freshman Trevor Lawrence.

Bryant had earned the job this fall with his improvement from a year ago.

"I'll tell you, I'm really proud of Kelly because man you have to have thick skin when you play quarterback and you got so many people with their opinions and agendas and they don't watch practice or tape," head coach Dabo Swinney said. "Even if they do, they don't know what they're watching. It's been a breath of fresh air because he's just been locked in on himself. He's had an awesome camp.

"In three scrimmages, he was 23 of 32 for 300-something yards, four touch- downs, and no interceptions. Did a tremendous job. He just came out on top from a grade standpoint."

However, the competition would continue into the regular season for the Tigers, with each player showing flashes of greatness—leaving the coaches to remain with the status quo.

"We want to continue to play both of them," Swinney said. "Trevor is a special talent. I think y'all see that. He's just going to get better. You've just got to love what you see out of Kelly. He's just locked in with what he's doing and is just trying to play well with his opportunity.

"I think both of these guys can help our football team."

That was until Saturday's game at Georgia Tech.

On a hot day in Atlanta, those watching the game appeared to have witnessed the official changing of the guard—with Lawrence becoming the man for the Tigers.

While Swinney had been quick in previous postgame meetings with the media to say that neither quarterback had done anything to change the status quo, following the Tigers' 49-28 victory over the Yellow Jackets Swinney was a little more vague with his response.

"He certainly played great," Swinney said. "We're going to enjoy it tonight. We're not going to set the depth chart here in the postgame press conference. We're going to celebrate a win, enjoy it and as coaches, we'll get back in the office tomorrow, evaluate and watch all the tape and go from there, just like we do every week."

"Great" may be an understatement for the play of Lawrence, as he completed 13- of-18 passes for 176 yards and four touchdowns—he also led the Tigers to five of their seven touchdowns (one coming on a Bryant-led drive and one coming on defense).

In fact, Lawrence's four touchdown passes was the the first four-touchdown pass- ing performance by a Clemson quarterback since Deshaun Watson on Nov. 26, 2016 (six vs. South Carolina) and he also became the first Clemson freshman to throw four touchdown passes since Watson on Sept. 27, 2014 (six vs. North Carolina).

The similarities to Watson were not just statistical.

On Lawrence's first touchdown pas of the day, which he rolled out to the left and threw a strike to wide receiver Hunter Renfrow, co-offensive coordinator Jeff Scott saw something very familiar.

"We had called a different play, and it was actually a check by him based on what he saw defensively," Scott said. "No. 1, being able to check it and identify it, and No. 2 being able to roll out of your left and make that play, that was a big-time throw. Obviously sprinting out to your left is harder than to your right. I will say it wasn't a surprise to see him do it. It's kind of become the expectation with him.

"It kind of reminded me of Deshaun's (Watson) check in his first game vs. Georgia. Big-time pressure coming. It wasn't a sprint out, but it was still a big throw and fitting that throw in there... to see that out of a true freshman is really special. I've been around 10 years and I sometimes reminisce when I see some plays."

When asked whether or not, based on his performance in the game, Lawrence had done enough to earn the starting job, Scott offered a strikingly similar response as Swinney.

"I think the way he played in his first two series he earned more opportunities today in the game, and he made the most of those," Scott said. "I think as coaches, this will be one of those videos that will be fun to go back and watch and grade and do all those things. We are going to enjoy this tonight and as coaches, we will got back and grade any decision that are made will be made after we grade the video."

Regardless of whether or not Lawrence is named the starting quarterback when the new depth chart is released Monday morning, one thing is certain—he is not going to stop working to help the Tigers win.

"I don't know. We'll see. I thought Kelly played a good game, too," Lawrence said. "I don't know what's going to happen. I'm just going to keep attacking every week and doing everything I can to help the team."

Lawrence to start

The second-ranked Clemson Tigers made it official, when it was announced by Clemson SID Ross Taylor that true freshman Trevor Lawrence has been named the Tigers' starting quarterback.

Lawrence played the best game of his young, four-game, career at Georgia Tech when he threw four touchdown passes and led the Tigers to touchdowns on five of the six possessions he was in the game.

However, the decision to make the change at quarterback was not the result of just one game—it was the totality of the body of work Lawrence had amassed that forced the Tigers' hand.

"It's just like we do every week. We sit down and have a staff meeting and we evaluate every player, every position, their performance," co-offensive coordinator Tony Elliott said. "And after four games, when you look at both of them, both of them have played well, done a lot for us, it just came down to you gotta reward productivity. If you look at his opportunities, he's taken advantage of them. Kelly didn't do anything wrong, it's just a situation where when he's been in the game he's been productive and to be fair to competition, just like we do at every position, coach decided to name him the starter for this game.

"Again, it's not a lifetime contract. He's got to prove it in practice, prove it in the next game and when Kelly gets his opportunities he'll have a chance to compete."

While many may think that the decision to tell a senior quarterback that led the Tigers to their third straight ACC title, a third straight appearance in the College Football Playoff and amassed a 12-2 record in his first year starting might be difficult, for Elliott is was not difficult at all because competition is part of the culture at Clemson.

"I'm not going to say it's difficult because that's the mindset and the culture that we have in place here at the program that these guys know that you have to bring it every single day," Elliott said. "They recognize the competition level, obviously Kelly is a guy who's done a lot for us, but he understood that he was going to have to compete. Same thing with Clelin (Ferrell) and Travis (Etienne) and Dexter Lawrence--they know every singe day that they come on this practice field and every single game they've got to be productive or somebody else is going to get a chance."

On the season, Lawrence has been on the field for a total of 24 drives—resulting in 13 touchdowns, two field goals, one fumble and five punts. Meaning, of the Tigers 163 total points scored this season, Lawrence has accounted for 97 of those points.

Elliott admitted that the decision came following a staff meeting Sunday night, and those production numbers played a big role in head coach Dabo Swinney making a change.

"It happened after we sat in with Coach Swinney in his staff meeting and we discussed it, but obviously you can't discount the production and the spark that he provided in that game," Elliott said. "But you go back to Texas A&M, Kelly was the guy that gave us the spark and we went with him because he had the hot-hand and obviously based on that he had the opportunity to start the next game.

"There was no collective decision where we were watching film. It was more everybody saying, we're four games in and both have played well, but let's look at the numbers and see how they pan out."

The biggest question is now: Is the job Lawrence's solely or will he be trading series' out with Bryant, as they did prior to this change. But that will be a decision for Swinney and quarterback's coach Brandon Streeter.

"That's like it is every week, Coach Swinney and Coach Streeter will sit down and determine how they want to manage that throughout the course of the game," Elliott said. "The biggest thing is, because of the production, coach did decide to give Trevor the opportunity and he's earned the opportunity based off his production to run out there first.

"Again it's week-to-week, so we'll still continue to evaluate the same way that we do, but obviously Trevor's earned that right to run out there first."

Players react to the change

On a unique day in Clemson, the announcement of the Tigers' coaching staff that incumbent quarterback Kelly Bryant had been benched and true freshman Trevor Lawrence would take over as the starting quarterback came to the media before the team was informed of the decision.

In fact, the only players who were told of the change were Bryant and Lawrence—leaving the other players to learn of the change at quarterback from the media because the team all had class before meeting as a group later in the afternoon.

"I didn't really have an opportunity to get in front of the team (at the time it was released). I just wanted to make sure we had an opportunity to talk to Kelly," head coach Dabo Swinney said. "We had some press things (previously scheduled), so I didn't get a chance until yesterday. I met with the senior group at 3:45. They understand."

The first player to learn of the change at quarterback Monday was starting running back Travis Etienne, who said that the change from Bryant to Lawrence would not change anything about the way the Tigers prepare.

"There was a change at quarterback," Etienne said. "Well, we have been having a rotation all season, so he is going to step in there and go in first, I guess. Nothing has changed. We are going to keep preparing the same way and keep rolling."

Wide receiver Amari Rodgers was happy to see Lawrence rewarded for the work that he put in, but, even in his excitement, he understands that the Tigers' unbeaten record is a tribute to both quarterbacks and the job that they have done through the first four games.

"I'm happy for him," Rodgers said. "He's been working his tail off since he got here. I am happy to see that it is paying off for him. He's been doing really good for us, Kelly has too. They both have.

"We're undefeated right now, so that's a credit to both of them."

For the players, there is an understanding that if they are going to believe in the saying, plastered all over the indoor facility, the football complex and the locker rooms, of "Best is the standard" the coaches much also practice what they preach.

And while this is the most visible demonstration of the coaches playing the best player, it is not the only instance where battles have occurred.

"It's no different than any other position," Swinney said. "We have seniors who are backups, juniors who are backups. It's competitive at every position. You have to earn it. It's a very competitive situation at quarterback. It's not like we have guys who can't win. We had Shaq Lawson and Vic Beasley at defensive end. They were very different but we played them both."

While it is not always easy, center Justin Falcinelli believes that Bryant understands why the Tigers made the move.

"Kelly understands how we do things," Falcinelli said. "He knows how we do things. He knows what to expect. He knows it. He is a great guy. We love them both. I don't care who is back there. I know they both can get the job done, so whoever is there first, it does not matter. They are both still good."

Bryant done at Clemson

Clemson head coach Dabo Swinney announced that quarterback Kelly Bryant has decided to transfer out of the program, and not play the remainder of the season after losing his starting job to true freshman Trevor Lawrence.

"Obviously saddened and disappointed that he's chosen to leave the team, but I really have absolutely nothing bad that I can say about Kelly Bryant,"He's one of the best young people I've ever been around, and even though I don't think this is a great

decision, I certainly respect it, and it doesn't change anything that I feel for Kelly. I love him, care about him. I wish him nothing but the best, and, again, sad that he has made this decision.

"All I can say is another program, wherever he decides to go, is going to get a quality quarterback and a very quality young man. We appreciate everything that Kelly gave to this program while he was here. He's a graduate, and like I said, he's one of the best young people you could ever be around. It's disappointing, but that's where we are, and something he decided that he felt like was best for him, so you have to respect that."

Swinney stated in Tuesday's press conference that, "I'm glad God ain't a coach. As a coach you have to be critical and you have to rank people. It's hard."

He reiterated that point during his weekly teleconference with the media.

As far as the decision, it's just -- you know, as a coach, sometimes you have to make tough decisions that are in the best interest of the team, and this is one of those decisions," Swinney said. "And I would make it all over again because I believe that it's what's right for our team, and I feel like Kelly would have continued to help us win and play a lot, but it's not what he wanted to do."

By choosing to leave before the fifth game, Bryant will be eligible to redshirt this season and he will have the opportunity to transfer following the 2018 season with one-year of eligibility left.

Swinney and the Clemson coaching staff could have eliminated that possibility if they had played him for even one down in Saturday's game against the Syracuse Orange, but that is not the way the Tigers' run their program.

"I certainly could have started him this week, which would have limited his options, but that's not how we operate here. That's not who we are," Swinney said. "So at the end of the day, it is what it is. I love Kelly. I wish him all the best. Again, I appreciate everything he's done for this University, this team, and respect his decision and wish him all the best.

Bryant announced to the Greenville News that he felt like the decision was a "slap the face" and that he was not given a "fair shot" to hold onto the starting job.

When asked about his feelings and whether or not he felt like Bryant was given a fair shot, Swinney stated that he disagrees with Bryant's opinion.

"Well, again, you know, he's totally entitled to his opinion. But absolutely I think we've given him a fair shot. I mean, I've always tried to be as open and honest and transparent as possible with Kelly throughout the process, as we are with all of our players. He won the job after Deshaun Watson, and he beat out the No. 1 quarterback in the country to do that in Hunter Johnson and another highly recruited quarterback in Zerrick Cooper, both of who have gone on to play elsewhere.

"He won the job, and he was the starter for us all last year and did a great job, and then he came out of camp slightly ahead, and so he continued to start these first four games.

"But like I said, I definitely feel like he's been given a fair shot. I don't think there's any question about that. But at the end of the day, this is not middle school. There's tough decisions that have to be made at this level, and you've got to do what's best for the team. I've had many, many players that have beaten out veterans over the years. Nuk Hopkins, when he came here in '09, after a couple games he was the best receiver and he beat out several veterans."

Bryant had started 18 games in his career, a 16-2 record, while throwing for 3,333 yards and 16 touchdowns in his career and led the Tigers to a third straight ACC title and third straight College Football Playoff appearance last season.

The biggest question now for the Tigers is: How will the team respond this week?

Waiting for the Tigers is a Syracuse team that not only beat the Tigers last season, but had their way with the them.

However, Swinney believes that the Tigers will be just fine moving forward because the players all understand the culture and competition.

"I don't think it'll affect us at all. I mean, everybody is disappointed," Swinney said. "Everybody -- these players understand competition. This is just -- players play, coaches coach. You don't always agree with decisions and things like that, but you get back to work. You take who you've got and you make the best of it, and that's exactly what we'll do.

"At the end of the day, again, everybody is making a big deal out of this because it's the quarterback. Like I said, this happens every year. I mean, there's a sophomore that beats out a senior or there's a freshman, an unbelievable rare freshman like a Nuk, a Sammy a Christian and Deshaun, a Mitch Hyatt, whatever, that walks in here and beats out a veteran guy. That happens every year, so this is not something that never happens. It just so happens that it's a quarterback this year."

GAME 5: SYRACUSE

It was an emotional start to a very stressful week for the head coach fo the second- ranked Clemson Tigers because Dabo Swinney had to tell his starting quarterback Kelly Bryant that he had lost his job to true freshman Trevor Lawrence.

"It's a bad day to be the head coach. Most days it's good. That was a bad day because I love Kelly," Swinney said of Monday's meeting. "It was emotional for him. Tough day. I gave him the day off last night. It was a rough afternoon. We don't get them here until 4 p.m. Brandon Streeter had already met with him Sunday. We met yesterday afternoon and it was emotional.

"He has played well. No guy who has ever been here has been more committed than Kelly Bryant. There is not a better leader. He's what you want your son to be like. I love him like a son. He's very disappointed. I don't have any doubt that he'll show up and go back to work and respond. It was tough."

While days like yesterday are not the ones that Swinney looks forward to, he understands that part of his job is to do whatever it takes to win football games—even if that means benching a quarterback that is 16-2, led your team to a third straight ACC title and an appearance the College Football Playoff.

"I hate being in that situation but that's my job," Swinney said. "My job is to critique, judge, evaluate, hold people accountable, be fair and do what's right. Doesn't make it easier, but where we are right now and what we're doing, it's what is right. It's just hard. It's tough. I always tell people, it doesn't always go our way and you just have to respond. When we have adversity, it can destroy you, define you or develop you. My hope is that it'll continue to develop Kelly into the player he can be and him becoming a better version of himself."

The Tigers will be in a unique situation with Bryant moving forward, as he could possibly sit out the remainder of the Tigers' games this season and, under the new red- shirt rules this year, redshirt this season and transfer to another school with one year to play.

Even though Swinney does not expect Bryant to go that route, he would not hold it against him if he chose to transfer.

"We talked about a lot of things. I won't get into details about our conversation. It was emotional," Swinney said. "If I were worried about that or deceitful, I could have told our coaches to make sure we start him against Syracuse to make sure he had five games in. But I'm not like that. It was a deep, long, emotional conversation. It was something we needed to talk through. If he walked in here today and said he didn't want to play unless needed, then that's what we'd do. I'd be disappointed, but I wouldn't judge him on that."

The emotional start to the week for the Tigers (4-0, 1-0 ACC) comes ahead of the stressful job of preparing for a Syracuse Orange (4-0, 1-0 ACC) that will try to accomplish a feat no ACC school has done in the last four seasons—beat the Tigers in consecutive seasons.

"We've got a huge challenge. It's a division game and there are two undefeated teams," Swinney said. "It's a huge game for both teams. They're coming in here confident. They beat us last year, so they know they can beat us. And we know that. It's going to take a much better performance by us to have a chance to beat them."

Even though revenge from last season's Friday the 13th loss to the Orange may be a motivating factor for the 85,000 fans that will fill Death Valley, the only motivation that Swinney has is knocking off the next team in their way of a fourth-straight division title.

"The idea of a bad memory and a bad taste, but no, we're not out to get revenge," Swinney said. "They won a game. They out-played us, out-coached us. This is a new season. When you look back on last year, you know, bad things happen. Let something define you, destroy you or develop you. We didn't lose another game last year until the Sugar Bowl. I think they lost five straight. Whether it's something great or bad, you have to move on.

"You can't say, 'I can't wait to get revenge 364 days from now.' You can't live like that. No, I'm not looking ahead. We want to win this game, but not because we lost last year. We want to win the division and be the best version of the 2018 team. They're in our way."

Brice is next man up

As soon as it was made official that quarterback Kelly Bryant was transferring from the Clemson Tigers football program, after losing his job to true freshman Trevor Lawrence, something else happened that many people did not notice—redshirt fresh- man Chase Brice got a promotion to backup quarterback.

"We definitely want to get Chase as much experience as we can," Swinney said prior to the Furman game. "He's going to be a great player here. Someone has to walk out there first. Don't say he's not a good player because he's third team. He's a very good player. Tavien Feaster is third team right now but he's pretty good. Pretty good. It's a good situation."

Brice, who has logged playing time in three of the Tigers' first four games this sea- son, has completed five of his eight pass attempts on the season for 37 yards and one interception. But even with his limited experience head coach Dabo Swinney was still very confident that Brice could win for the Tigers.

"Chase Brice--who's he's just kind of a gunslinger," Swinney said. "He's a winner, incredible job on scout team last year, he's tough, he's savvy, he's got an excellent arm, great instincts for the game. Again, he's been a big-time winner his whole life."

However, it is not only Swinney who sees the potential for Brice to step up to the challenge of being the backup quarterback for the second-ranked team in the country —his position coach has seen the leadership since he recruited him.

"I love Chase Brice. He's a great kid. He's got a demeanor that's similar to Kelly Bryant as far as personality," Streeter said. "Everybody on the team loves the guy. He can get along with anybody. He's just that type of person. I think his leadership quality is unbelievable. His talent, just watching him in recruiting him and then watching him in preseason camp and throughout the year when we had different opportunities to watch him - especially during scrimmages in bowl prep - he's got what it takes."

"He's got the arm strength. He can move. He's big. He's smart and he under- stands the big picture. He's learning the system this fall and that was a big challenge for him. He's got to take every day and get better and not take any day for granted. If he didn't do that then he wouldn't be where he is right now. He's starting to understand the offense a lot better and I feel really good about Chase."

The Tigers had better feel "really good" about Brice because the Tiger quarterback room is one of the smallest in the country—with only Lawrence, Brice and, late- scholarship offer, Ben Batson remaining as the only scholarship quarterbacks.

However, Swinney's program has been built on the idea of "next man up".

Whether it was last season when Deshaun Watson was no longer on the team or when Greg Huegel was lost to a season ending injury or this season, when Bryant announced that he would be transferring, it has been and always will be "Next man up."

"That is why it is so important that you are always developing that guy who maybe is not playing right now," Swinney said. "But his time is going to come at some point. You have to be patient, and I think that is what we do best around here. We believe in developing our guys. I have never signed a junior college guy. I have always signed high school guys and we bring them here and we develop them

The Game

After an emotional week for the second-ranked Clemson Tigers, they got all they could handle and more from the Syracuse Orange Saturday, as they survived a scare and escaped with a 27-23 victory behind the play of backup quarterback Chase Brice.

"Hat's off to Syracuse, what unbelievable fight," head coach Dabo Swinney said. "At the end of the day, I'm just so proud of our team and our staff. Challenges within the week, within the game, but I am so proud of our team.

"I have been a part of some great wins as a head coach, been a part of some great ones as a player, as an assistant coach—but this is one that I will never forget."

The Tigers played from behind nearly the entire game until the final drive of the game, when they put together an incredible 13-play, 94-yard drive that was capped off by Travis Etienne's third touchdown of the day.

"Our ability to run the ball (was the key to this win)," Swinney said. ""I told Tony (Elliott) and Jeff (Scott), boys, we going to have to do this the old fashioned way and somewhere Danny Ford and Gene Stallings are probably drinking a beer because that was old school....In the long run, this will be a defining moment for this team."

The Orange opened the scoring, as quarterback Eric Dungy led them on an 11- play, 58-yard drive that was capped off by a 35-yard field goal by Andre Szmyt that gave the Orange a 3-0 lead.

Lawrence's first series came to a quick end. After finding Tee Higgins for a 19- yard gain on his first play as a starter, the Tigers gave the ball right back to the Orange on a fumbled exchange between Lawrence and running back Travis Etienne.

The Orange were unable to advance the ball, as they settled for second field goal of the day that extended the lead to 6-0.

The third drive of the game was the charm, as Lawrence led the Tigers on a 10- play, 60-yard touchdown drive that was capped off when, behind the "Jumbo Package" that features defensive linemen Christian Wilkins and Dexter Lawrence, running back Travis Etienne took a direct snap and dove for the 1-yard touchdown.

After the Tigers missed a 48-yard field goal, the Orange needed only six plays, that featured a 51-yard throw-and-catch from Dungy to Tajh Harris, and a 1-yard touchdown run by Dungy to finish off a drive that gave the Orange a 13-7 lead.

On the Tigers' ensuing drive, the worst possible thing that could happen for the second-ranked Clemson Tigers happened in Saturday's game, as starting quarterback Trevor Lawrence was injured when he attempted to roll out to his left and took a shot to the upper body on third down.

"He's really doing great, he actually wanted to come back and play. He had concussion-like symptoms," Swinney said. "He was like, 'I'm good to go.' He was trying to come back in the game, but they (medical staff) shut him down.

"He was celebrating to with his teammates after the game."

Following a Tiger punt the Orange added to their lead, as Dungy once again led the Orange on a scoring drive—this time it was a third field goal of the day that extended the lead to 16-7.

Behind backup quarterback Chase Brice, the Tigers cut the lead to 16-10 after Greg Huegel connected on a 43-yard field goal that finished off an 8-play, 55-yard drive that took 2:46 off the clock.

Following the Orange's first turnover of the game, an interception by A.J. Terrell, the Tigers cut into the Orange lead. The Tigers gained only 5 yards before another field goal by Huegel cut the Orange lead to 16-13.

The Tiger defense forced the third punt of the third quarter, however return man Amari Rodgers muffed the punt and the Orange recovered the ball at the Clemson 10- yard line.

The Orange needed all four downs to extend the lead to 10 points, after Dungy leapt over the line for the touchdown that gave the Orange a 23-13 lead.

The Tigers' answered with their best drive of the day. The Tigers went 75 yards in only six plays, and after Etienne's 25-yard touchdown run they cut the lead to 23-20..

Tiger Tracks:

Clemson was without two starters, cornerback Mark Fields and kick returner/ wide receiver Cornell Powell.

Wide receiver Hunter Renfrow reach the historic mark with his 150th reception in the first quarter.

Travis Etienne had his third-straight 100-yard game, as he amassed a career-high 203 yards on 27 carries, including three touchdowns.

Coaches Corner:

Co-offensive coordinator on the fourth-and-6 pass that Chase Brice completed to Tee Higgins to keep the Tigers' go-ahead drive alive.

"I'll never forget that fourth-and-6 pass form Brice, where he threaded the needle, about 3 yards wide, to Tee Higgins, and without that pass, we don't win the game."

Player Perspective:

Chase Brice on the fourth-and-6 pass that kept the Tigers' game-winning drive alive.

"It was a no-brainer. We had the momentum and our defense did a great job getting the ball back. We decided to throw and we just made the play."

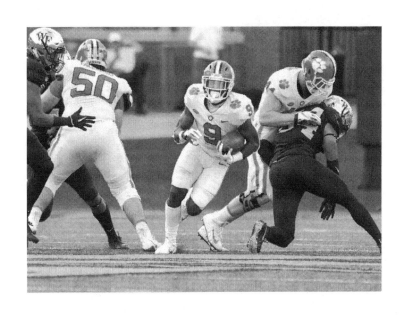

GAME 6: WAKE FOREST

This season, the Tigers' undefeated record can be attribute, at least in large part to their success on the ground.

Through 5 games, the Tigers ranks 20th in yards per game (ahead of Alabama and Ohio State), 10th in avg. (ahead of Alabama, Ohio State and Georgia), and T-15 with UGA in touchdowns (ahead of Alabama).

For the Tigers, it is this kind of running game that opens up the rest of their offense.

"That goes back forever and ever and ever," head coach Dabo Swinney said. "When you can run the football and have a quarterback and people on the outside that you can throw and catch with and you have the chance to create some kind of balance that is the ultimate goal for any offensive philosophy.

"Our ability to run the ball creates everything in the play action game. It dictates the type of coverage we want to create big play potential. It helps us take advantage of our skill outside. If forces defenses to have to give you matchups to get extra hats in the box to stop the run so it's big."

That ability to create matchup issues for defenses showed up in a big way in Saturday's 27-23 victory over Syracuse, as the Tigers amassed 293 yards on the ground.

"Really proud of the way that we continued to run the ball," co-offensive coordinator Jeff Scott said. "I believe that we had 293 yards this week, and I think the last three games we've averaged 283 yards rushing--which is awesome. I think that's just going to open up some things in the passing game and create some issues for defenses trying to figure out how they want to defend us.

"We had 13 explosive plays--nine of them in the running game, which I think was really big."

On the final game-winning drive, the Tigers rushed for 79 yards on the ground. But making the feat more impressive was the fact that the Tigers ran the ball even when the Syracuse defense knew it was coming.

"I was proud of our running backs being able to go and impose our will," Scott said. "It's one thing to be able to run the ball--it's another thing to run the ball when they know you're running the ball because that is very difficult."

Etienne for Heisman:

The bulk of the work on the ground this season has belonged to sophomore Travis Etienne—who has amassed 594 yards this season, while averaging 8.4 yards per carry and has found the end zone eight times.

Etienne, who was named the ACC's "Running Back of the Week" for his performance on Saturday, amassed career highs in rushing attempts (27), rushing yards (203) and rushing touchdowns (three) and recorded

Clemson's first 200-yard rushing performance since Andre Ellington in the 2012 season opener.

When asked whether or not Etienne deserved consideration for the Heisman Trophy, Scott gushed over the sophomore.

"He's special. I wouldn't want to trade him for anybody else in the country," Scott said. "I mean, I think he's awesome. It's obvious to everybody watching the game, seeing him breaking tackles and he just gets better and better. Part of it with him too, is he's got to learn to stick with some runs because a lot of them he wants to bounce. He's also getting coached up to go hit it and get the first down and not always go for the home run. He's not one we want to slow down a whole lot. He's having a great year and we're not surprised."

Bonding over breakfast

Clemson head coach Dabo Swinney addressed concerns with the locker room after Saturday's 27-23 victory over

the Syracuse Orange by sharing a little known fact—
that defensive lineman Christian Wilkins took newly
named starting quarterback

Trevor Lawrence to breakfast Wednesday after the team
learned that former starting quarterback Kelly Bryant
had left the team.

"I saw unbelievable leadership this week," Swinney
said. "Christian, a simple thing, took Trevor to breakfast
Wednesday morning. You know, just took him to breakfast on his own. I didn't know about it. Somebody sent a
picture to me saying, hey coach, I just want you to know
the type of leaders you have on your team. There is a
random picture and Christian taking Trevor to
breakfast.

"That's the type of leadership we've got. It's inspiring.
It's inspiring to see young people, especially, rally and
believe and hang in there and stay together," Swinney
said. "And as I said, these are things, these are lessons

that they will carry with them the rest of their life, you know, because I really think a lot of things that you learn inside the lines you take with them outside the lines, into your life. You have things go against you, but it's just how you respond. These guys responded in a very emotional way today."

That breakfast was a result of Wilkins "paying it forward" because he remembers a time when he was the young, inexperienced lineman who was in need of guidance.

"Really it was just kind of enjoying a meal. I'll do that for anyone on the team. Any of the young guys, or anyone period, who seem like they have a lot on their plate. A lot of my teammates have done it for me, so I just like to show my teammates that I've got their back regardless of anything."

"We had to hit it early, that's why we went to breakfast-- before anybody was out and about. Some people still saw us, it wasn't that big of a deal..I was just on a date with a cute blonde."

On Monday, it was shared that not only did Wilkins treat the young superstar to breakfast, but Lawrence paid the generosity forward, as he took the offensive line to breakfast Friday.

"He earned the (starting job)," offensive lineman Gage Cervenka said. "It's not like we just gave it to him. He earned up and been working for it. He's a great kid. What shows character with Trevor, he actually took out the offensive line to breakfast.

Friday morning. He's a great player. We tell him hey you're the guy. You got the keys and just drive the car and let's go. We've got his back with everything."

Wilkins believes that it is that kind of camaraderie that ensured that the Tigers did not lose their focus with the departure of Bryant last week.

"I wasn't worried at all. Obviously, it was a tough situation, but we didn't really think of it because everyone still has a job to do," Wilkins said. "We've all got to be professional. Everyone has to do their part and that was kind of the mindset. Whatever goes on, whether it's outside world or the visiting team, you show up when you're playing football and you've got.a job to do."

The Game

The No. 4 Clemson Tigers moved to 6-0 (3-0 ACC) for the sixth time in eight years with their 63-3 victory over the Wake Forest Demon Deacons (3-3, 0-2 ACC) Saturday in a historic performance in front of a mostly orange BB&T Stadium in Winston-Salem.

"Really proud of our team, probably our most complete game of the season heading into the open week," head coach Dabo Swinney said. "Our goal was to put it together completely and we did that.

"It's a good start to October, so it's always nice to head into the open week with a win...I didn't know that the score would be 63-3. I really felt like we would play our best game this week and we did that. Had a great week of practice and thought this was a game we could make a statement with."

On the day, the Tigers amassed 471 rushing, fourth all-time in rushing totals—which gave the Tigers more than 1,000 yards rushing in a four game span, the first time the Tigers accomplished that feat since the first four games of last season, and it marked the fourth consecutive game the Tigers gained more than 200 yards, the first time since the 2015 season.

"Man, I was so pleased with our ability to run the ball. thats what every team dreams of when it comes to running the ball," Swinney said."We've been really explosive—which we didn't have last year. Then you throw in the fact that we have been so explosive in the run game—I'm just really proud of our team.'

After a slow start to the game, in which both teams combined for five punts and a Tiger fumble, the Tigers broke the stalemate, as Tiger running back Travis Etienne (167 yards on 10 carries and three touchdowns) took a handoff on the first-play of the fourth drive and went 59 yards for the touchdown.

After both teams exchanged punts, the Tigers went back to work on the ground. Led by Tavien Feaster and Etienne, the Tigers marched down the field to the Demon Deacons' 28-yard line. On fourth-and-1 from the 28, Etienne broke free for a 22-yard gain and, two plays later, scored from 3 yards out that extended the lead to 14-0.

The Tigers' continued to pile on in the first half, as they needed only five plays and 2:16 off the clock to go 75 yards after Trevor Lawrence (20-25 for 175 yards, two touchdowns and no interceptions) found fellow true freshman Justyn Ross for a 55- yard touchdown.

Lawrence was not finished in the first half, as he found Tee Higgins for a 20-yard touchdown that capped off a 10-play, 81-yard drive that took 2:57 off the clock and ex- tended the lead to 28-0.

The Tigers continued to pile on the Demon Deacons in the second half. After the Tigers forced the seventh punt of the game, they began their opening drive of the half at their own 30-yard line.

The Tigers needed only one-play, as Etienne took a handoff from Lawrence and went 70 yards in 10 seconds for his third touchdown of the day that gave the Tigers a 35-0 lead.

The Demon Deacons finally ended the shutout on their next possession, after starting quarterback Sam Hartman was pulled for backup Kendall Hinton. The Demon Deacons went 72 yards on seven plays before their drive stalled at the Clemson 7- yard line, and were forced to settle for a 25-yard field goal.

The Tigers answered the Demon Deacon score. Behind backup quarterback Chase Brice the Tigers needed only four combined plays and touchdown runs of 70 yards by Adam Choice and 65 yards by true freshman Lyn-J Dixon to extend the lead to 49-3.

The Tigers added two final scores, as Brice found Diondre Overton in the end zone from 2 yards out, and Dixon found the end zone for the second time on a 52-yard run that extended the lead to 63-3.

Tiger Tracks:

Trevor Lawrence became only the fourth freshman QB to throw for double-digit touchdowns in program history.

Travis Etienne became the first Clemson player to rush for at least three touchdowns in consecutive games since Travis Zachery against Duke (four) and Georgia Tech (three) in 1999.

The number of 50-plus-yard rushing touchdowns by the Tigers Saturday: five. The number of 50-plus-yard rushing touchdowns in 15 games by the national champion 2016 Clemson Tigers: one.

Clemson had three players reach the 100-yard rushing mark in a single game for only the sixth time in school history. It's the program's first time accomplishing the feat since Sept. 30, 2006, vs. Louisiana Tech (Davis, Spiller, Chancellor).

The Tiger played four quarterbacks in the game, including true freshman Ben Batson and wide receiver Hunter Renfrow, who competed a pass to Dabo Swinney's son Will.

Coaches Corner:

Dabo Swinney on whether or not true freshman Lyn-J Dixon earned more playing time:

"There's only one ball...You want to take Travis out? There is only one ball."

THE BYE WEEK

ESPN College GameDay analyst Desmond Howard had some harsh words for the No. 3 Clemson Tigers during their win at Wake Forest, in which he called the Tigers a "finesse' offense.

"I don't see them being a physical outfit offensively. They are more of a fitness group," Howard said. "They are not gonna be a smash mouth group. You can't change who you are in the middle of the season. You are who you are. You are what you are. I think the quarterback situation is gonna catch up with them and the defense hasn't been as dominant as people have anticipated with that four defensive linemen all NFL caliber studs.

"It will catch up with them at some point. I think they are gonna lose a regular season game and maybe the ACC Championship game."

The Tigers did all they could to prove Howard wrong in Saturday's 63-3 rout of the Wake Forest Demon Deacons.

In the game, the Tigers amassed 698 yards of offense, the fifth-most in a game in school history, averaged 10.0 yards per play and eclipsed the 400-yard rushing mark for the first time since rushing for 416 against Miami (Fla.) on Oct. 24, 2015.

The Tigers also gained 471 rushing yards are the fourth-most yards on the ground in program history and the most since Oct. 31, 1981 when the Tigers amassed 536 rushing yards against Wake Forest and averaged 11.8 yards per carry, breaking the previous school record set on Oct. 17, 1903 against Georgia Tech (11.2).

All of which left the coaching staff with big smiles on their faces after the game.

"I'm not a big stats guy. Proud of the numbers, and really I'm proud because I see the smiles on faces of our young men," co-offensive coordinator Tony Elliott said. "We still got a lot of room to improve. Nowhere near where we want to be with our third down percentage. To come out of the gate and fumble the ball and put our defense in a bind, there's still a lot of things we can improve. I was just happy the guys got a glimpse to see what they're capable of."

When asked about the comments that Howard made about the Tigers' offense, head coach Dabo Swinney took the high-road—admitting that the people in those positions are paid to create some controversy.

"I guess someone has to be the bad guy and the good guy," Swinney said. "Those guys have a job to do. They have to create some storylines. But we've been able to run the football all year. We are not a finished product by any stretch of the imagination."

While Swinney took the politically correct approach, his co-offensive coordinator Jeff Scott was clearly upset with the comments that were made about the Tigers.

"I think over the past three games we've averaged over 300 rushing yards per game," Scott said. "We had three backs over 125 yards rushing. Maybe somebody can send that to Desmond Howard so he can get his facts straight. It's hard to be a finesse group when you are rushing for 300 yards a game. You would agree with that, wouldn't you?"

The Tigers finished the game reaching the 300-yard mark for the second-time this season (309 vs. Georgia Southern). Clemson reached the 300-yard rushing mark twice last year and has now posted multiple 300-yard rushing games in back-to-back seasons for the first time since 2006 (four) and 2007 (two),

Of Clemson's 471 rushing yards, 310 came via five touchdown runs of 50 yards or more, but the scary thing for opposing defenses is that Swinney believes this team has yet to play their best football.

"We had a couple of miscues early, like dropped passes and bad timing on snaps, but it's just some small things that we have to continue to iron out," Swinney said. "We're going to play some teams where those mistakes will cost us. We are still a work in progress, but we can run the ball.

"Like I told everyone in the preseason camp, our running backs are going to be special. I think they can be some of the best in the country,"

ETN for Heisman

The No. 4 Clemson Tigers may have a Heisman candidate on their team—and it is not who many had thought it would be.

Entering the 2018 season, the Tigers had two players squarely on the radar of the Heisman watch pundits—senior quarterback Kelly Bryant and true freshman quarterback Trevor Lawrence.

While Bryant is no longer on the team and Lawrences career is only just beginning, a third candidate has emerged through the first six games of the season—sophomore running back Travis Etienne, who is quickly jumping up the Tiger record books and taking his place as one of the nation's best running backs.

"All of that stuff is to be determined but I know this, he is playing as good as anybody in the country after six games," head coach Dabo Swinney said of Etienne during his weekly call-in show.

In only six games of work this season, Etienne ranks seventh in FBS rushing yards per game (126.83) , sixth in average yards per rush (9.17), fourth in rushing yds (761), fourth in rushes of 10 yds or more (23), third in rushes of 20 yards or more (10), fourth in rushes of 30 yards or more (five) and sixth in rushes of 40 yards or more (three)—all while ranking 67th in attempts per game (13.83).

"(Clemson SID) Ross (Taylor) was telling me the other day he is like top five in everything but, has 40 less attempts than the guy that is leading," Swinney said. "He has been incredibly productive and efficient. His yards per carry are off the charts."

Even with those numbers Swinney understands that they do not award the Heisman Trophy after six games.

"Now six games, I don't think wins a Heisman, but you never know. He's got a chance," Swinney said. "If he can find a way to get another 100 yards in this next game then he will tie a school record that I think has been there for a long time.

"He has already broken the school record for rushing yards in a four-game span. He did that last week."

Etienne became the first Clemson player to rush for a touchdown in six straight games since Wayne Gallman's eight-game streak to end the 2016 season. He also now has six career games with multiple rushing touchdowns. He has now recorded back- to-back games with multiple rushing touchdowns for the second time in his career (vs. Florida State and The Citadel in 2017).

Etienne became the first Clemson player to rush for 100 yards in four straight games since Woodrow Dantzler against Wake Forest, Virginia, Duke and NC State in 2000. He is one 100-yard game shy of the school record of five consecutive 100-yard rushing games, set by Kenny Flowers in 1985 and by Raymond Priester in 1996-97.

And in last week's 63-3 victory over Wake Forest alone, Etienne eclipsed the number of rushing touchdowns of 50 yards or more accrued in 15 games by the 2016 national champion Clemson squad, which recorded only one rushing touchdown that season.

"Travis is playing as good as anybody in the country<" Swinney said. "We've had a couple of games where he probably could have rushed for 400 by himself if we left him in there.

"He has been so efficient."

Tigers focused on themselves

When your offense is putting up numbers at an almost historic rate, one might think that a bye week would be a chance to relax—but that was not the case for the fourth-ranked Clemson Tigers.

Instead, they went to work trying to find ways to become even more dynamic than they already are on offense.

"The biggest thing is just our precision and execution," co-offensive coordinator Tony Elliott said. "Obviously, I felt like our guys were headed in the right direction, but we just didn't execute with the precision that we needed to. We still have to improve on third down, obviously we've been either hot or cold--some games have been good, some games have been bad. The biggest thing is looking at our alignments, our structure--just making sure that we're not tipping things because you've got six games of information that people are looking at.

"So, just challenging our guys to make sure that we're not just getting comfortable just running what we run because that's what we run, but being able to change it up a little bit and disguise some things. Again, as you go through the stretch, the next half of the season, guys are really going to start honing in on the details of alignments, splits, all those kind of things."

The Tigers did not use their extra week only on themselves, instead they also got in some much needed work on their next opponent—the No. 15 N.C. State Wolfpack (5-0, 2-0 ACC).

"And (we got) a good head start on N.C. State-- evaluating their personal, structure, reviewing the games that we've played them over the last couple of years because they've been competitive games," Elliott said. "So, just making sure that we've got a good head start on what they do."

While the Wolfpack have to replace nine defensive starters off last year's defense , they have still been able to piece together a squad that ranks 32nd in total defense, 16th in scoring defense, t-15 in rush defense and 84th in pass defense because of a high-level of recruiting.

"You've gotta give those guys credit--they work their butts off in recruiting and they're a top-10 program," Elliott said. "In their defense, you don't see much of a drop- off. I know on paper they don't have a lot of returning starters, but all of those guys on the front four have played a lot of football--with the exception of one freshman.

"They have done a really, really good job of recruiting--they recruit to their system. They know what they want to do on defense and the mix of guys that have experience from last year means they're very, very confident."

The Tigers and the Wolfpack have played in instant classic games each of the last two season's—with the Tigers winning each of the games by a combined 14 points, each win coming by a touchdown.

And even though the Wolfpack are searching for their first victory over the Tigers in six years, the Tigers are certain they will get their best shot from the Wolfpack.

"They are going to come in confident, ready to play," Elliot said. "They've played us well the last couple of years, but what I remember the last time they were in the valley is they played us tough. Now, we gave them some opportunities. We turned the ball over three times in the red zone, we fumbled on the 1, we got stopped on a fourth- and-1 with Deshaun, we had a pick-six, so we gave them some opportunities to stay in the game."

Regardless of whether or not the Tigers had a bye week to prepare for the challenge of facing a Wolfpack team that is hungry for revenge, they understand the game will be won by the team that executes the best.

"I'm pretty sure they did the same thing (during their bye week). I don't think the off-week gave us an advantage because they had an off-week as well," Elliott said. "I'm pretty sure that they went through a similar process of trying to break any tendencies that they have, but most important it's going to come down to what it always comes down to in games like this: Which team can come out and execute with precision at a high level?"

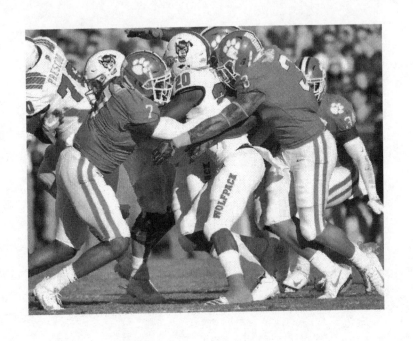

GAME 7: N.C. STATE

The fourth-ranked Clemson Tigers defense had their hands full when the No. 15 N.C. State Wolfpack came to town.

Led by senior quarterbacks Ryan Finley, the Wolfpack are averaging 480.2 yards of offense—including 335.3 passing yards, which ranks fourth in the FBS, and 144.8 yards rushing—which means the Tigers will have to be at their best if they want to keep their undefeated record in tact this week.

"He is just really good at what he does," defensive coordinator Brent Venables said. "He is accurate, poised, tough. He has good quickness. He certainly takes what is there, but he is very aggressive and is very confident.

"He will throw the seam when there is not really a hole there. He does a great job immediately understanding the positioning of a route and throwing the ball where it needs to be based on where you are at. He is very good with what he does."

However, outside of a week 2 performance which saw Texas A&M quarterback Kellan Mond slice up the Tiger defense for 430 passing yards, the Tigers have done fairly good against the pass—considering their inexperience in the secondary at the start of the season.

Even with the 430-yard performance by Mond, the Tigers still rank sixth in the FBS in pass defense, allowing only 152.8 yards per game through the air.

In fact, the Tigers held the ACC's third-leading passer, Wake Forest's Sam Hartman, to only seven completions on 20 attempts for 74 yards and one interception. But Venables understands the difference in playing a true freshman (Hartman) and a senior are night and day.

"They definitely have RPOs like Wake Forest does and everybody does, but it is a different system and a different quarterback," Venables said. "Sam s a terrific player and he has a great future ahead of him, but he does not know what he does not know yet. Where this week is a much different challenge where he is 23 or 24 years old and has played a lot of football. He (Finley) has a lot of experience and is a very talented player."

If there is any doubt that the Tigers will get the Wolfpack's best shot this weekend, Venables quickly dismissed the idea, but added that he believes that getting everyones best shot is something the Tigers have grown accustomed to and enjoy.

"I expect every week to play a team that's passionate group of guys that treat us like it's the biggest game of the year," Venables said. "I think it's a compliment to our guys, and to me that's how I try to coach. To me that's the only way to coach—with great intensity, coach with great passion and great toughness.

"But they don't need for me to show them, they have great respect for N.C. State. N.C. State's given us everything they've got the last few years and this year won't be any different...We love big games where there's a lot at stake and I think the bigger the games the better our guys play."

Doeren plans to hit Lawrence

The Clemson Tigers and the N.C. State Wolfpack have had their fair share of chippy games the last couple of seasons.

Whether it was Tiger offensive lineman Isaiah Battle taking a swing at a Wolfpack player, members of the Wolfpack coaching staff taking swings at former quarterback Deshaun Watson or the Wolfpack head coach Dave Doeren praising the fact that the Wolfpack knocked former Tiger running back Wayne Gallman out of the game two years ago, the Tigers and the Wolfpack have no love lost.

However, Wolfpack head coach Dave Doeren stated that his team's goal is to once again put the Tigers' best player on his back.

"We have to swarm and we have to strike and have a bad attitude when we get there. We've done that in the past," Doeren said during his weekly radio show. "What do you do? You hit him. You try to get him out of rhythm, you try to make him see things he hasn't seen and you have to make plays.Rattle him a little bit. He hasn't been rattled. He has made plays and he is a good football player and he has great talent around him.

"But if you can just get him to question what he's looking at a little bit, give the D-line a little bit more time to get there and the blitzes a little more time to get there and get him on his back more than he wants to be on his back."

Not Christmas cards

Needless to say the Clemson Tigers and the N.C. State Wolfpack are not exchanging Christmas cards after their last couple of games.

Not only have the games been incredibly close, with each of the last two games being decided by seven points, there has been some gamesmanship—and down-right dirty play—on both sides.

Most recent, last year saw former Wolfpack defensive lineman Bradley Chubb taking towels from players and head coach Dave Doeren accusing the Clemson staff of cheating for their social media department's use of a laptop on the sideline.

But even with the events of recent years—Swinney and Doeren are friends, but fierce competitors.

"You said coaches alleging laptops, I haven't alleged any laptops," Swinney said with a laugh. "Dave sent me some Adidas towels back and apologized. I'm like these are Adidas, these aren't even our (Nike) towels. So I guess Bradley Chubb still has them hung up in his apartment in Denver somewhere.

"It's an incredibly competitive game for both teams, but we have had some crazy stuff though. Y'all remember (former Clemson offensive lineman) Isaiah Battle punched some guy at the the game one year. Oh my god. He lost his mind. And then we had one of their coaches push Deshaun Watson one year. I had to call him and apologize for Isaiah, and he had so call me and apologize for his coach pushing Deshaun."

"Last year, I don't really understand the laptop stuff, I'm not sure -- but you know. It's all good. I get along fine with Dave."

The Game

The No. 3 Clemson Tigers turned the biggest game in the ACC this season into one of their best moments, as they dismantled the No. 15 N.C. State Wolfpack by a final score of 41-7 on a Homecoming Saturday inside Death Valley.

"really proud of our team—all three phases. I feel like that's two games in a row now," Clemson head coach Dabo Swinney said. "Just a complete performance and I thought it was a dominant game. The second largest margin of victory against a ranked opponent. We wanted to put together a complete performance and that's what we did.

"Really a complete game, we didn't win the division— but at least we control our own destiny and we knew that was what the winner was going to be able to say."

In a dominant effort, the Wolfpack offense was held to a season-low 297 total yards, 193 passing yards and 104 rushing yards against a Tiger defense that proved to be up to the challenge of facing an upset minded Wolfpack team.

"Defensively it was a dominant performance," Swinney said. "I thought our defense was awesome. Stopped them on downs, three turnovers...I really sensed that we were going to play a great game. I sensed that our guys wanted to play this game on Monday, so my job was to keep them dialed down a little."

The Tigers opened the scoring on the opening drive of the game for the first time this season, as Travis Etienne's 3-yard touchdown run capped off a nine-play, 57-yard

drive. On the drive, Tiger quarterback Trevor Lawrence (26-39 for 309 yards, one touchdowns and no interceptions) found Hunter Renfrow and Tee Higgins twice for a combined 35 yards.

After both teams exchanged punts, the Tigers went back to work. The Tigers drive started on their own 25 yard line when Wolfpack head coach Dave Doeren declined a holding penalty on second-and-8 that would have forced the Tigers to go 18 yards in two plays. The Tigers capitalized on the decision, as they needed only two plays—including a 46-yard touchdown pass from Lawrence to Higgins—to add their second touchdown of the day.

Following a botched fake field goal for the Tigers, the Wolfpack had their best drive of the game—as they reached the Tigers' 42-yard line. But on third-and-10, quarterback Ryan Finley fumbled the snap and the ball was recovered by the Tigers with 2:15 to play in the first half.

Following the turnover, the Tigers added to their lead on Etienne's second touchdown of the day that capped the seven-play, 54-yard drive.

The Tigers were not through in the first half. On the Wolfpack's next possession, Finley's pass was intercepted by K'Von Wallace and returned 46 yards to the Wolfpack 4-yard line. The Tigers settled for a field goal and closed the first half of play up 24-0.

After both teams exchanged a combined three punts, the Tigers once again added to their lead. After the Wolfpack attempted a fake punt that was unsuccessful, the Tigers took over at the Wolfpack 22-yard line. The four-play drive culminated in Clemson history, as Etienne became the first player in Clemson history to rush for three touchdowns in three straight games.

The Wolfpack finally broke the shutout in the fourth quarter, as Reggie Gallaspy capped a 10-play, 75-yard drive with a 9-yard touchdown that cut the lead to 34-7.

The Wolfpack tried their second trick-play of the day on the ensuing kick off, when they attempted an onside kick that was recovered by the Tigers at the 50-yard line.

The Tigers added to their lead after kicker Greg Huegel connected on his second field goal of the day.

After the Wolfpack's sixth punt of the day, the Tigers' turned to backup quarterback Chase Brice.

On his first drive of the day, Brice completed all three of his passes for 56 yards before the Tigers turned true freshman Lyn-J Dixon loose on the Wolfpack, as Dixon rushed for 25 yards—including a 2-yard touchdown run.

After scoring 104 points in their last two games, Swinney believes this offensive group has the opportunity to be one of his most memorable.

"I think we have the opportunity to be a special group on offense. Our ability to run the football creates problems," Swinney said. "It forces people to commit to something defensively. I'm really pleased where our offense is.

Players Perspective

Travis Etienne was very impressed with the performance of his true freshman quarterback Trevor Lawrence, who threw for a career-high 309 yards in Saturday's win.

"He showed me what he has been showing me that he is a player," Etienne said. "Big-time players make big-time plays in big-time games and that is exactly what he did. He just came out here and was just Trevor."

Tigers Tracks

Tee Higgins set a career high with eight receptions through and added 109 yards through the air.

Clemson forced a takeaway in a 15th consecutive contest, the program's longest streak since a 15-game stretch across the 2012-13 seasons.

GAME 8: FLORIDA STATE

The No. 2 Clemson Tigers (7-0, 4-0 ACC) were looking to start the season 8-0 for the seventh time in school history, and the third time in the last four seasons, this when they travel to Doak Campbell Stadium to take on the Florida State Seminoles (4- 3, 2-3 ACC).

While the Seminoles have struggled to put together a finished product under first-year head coach Willie Taggart, but Clemson head coach Dabo Swinney understands that it takes some time before teams begin to play to their ability after a coaching change.

"It's hard. It speaks to what happened in the first few games," Swinney said. "They want to be tempo. They play fast and try to create space and one-on-ones. That's different from who they were. It has taken them time to hit their stride. The Virginia Tech game got away from them. Samford came in there with a hot quarterback and a good plan. Their quarterback is a baller. They hit some big plays on them, but FSU ended up winning. Syracuse just got to their quarterback and that was the biggest issue in that game.

According to the recruiting websites, the Seminoles have out-recruited the Tigers every year since Swinney became head coach in 2009.

For Swinney, that means that even though this isn't the same Florida State in terms of their record—it is the same Florida State in terms of their talent.

"Those first few games, they were figuring out who could do what," Swinney said. "They have really settled in since. They were right there in a position to win the Miami game and led most of the game. They're 3-1 in their last four. Records don't matter. If records mattered, Purdue wouldn't have defeated Ohio State. We lost to Syracuse last year and they won three games. That stuff doesn't matter. That's why you have to prepare and respect every opponent. If you don't think they've got talent, you're not paying attention. If recruiting rankings mean something, we're 1-9 against them."

However, the Tigers are not 1-9 against the Seminoles. In fact, Swinney and this senior class will be looking for their fourth straight victory over the Seminoles—something he believes would be a big accomplishment for a program that has only beaten the Seminoles seven times in the history of the program.

"That would be big. This is a prideful group aware of opportunities they have outside of our team goals," Swinney said. "They have goals within goals. No other ACC team has done that. It would a great accomplishment for that group."

A big part to what this Tiger team has been able to accomplish this season has been a direct result of the sheer number of players the Tigers have that can contribute.

By comparison, last week, the Alabama Crimson Tide played 44 players in their blowout over an unranked Tennessee team, the Oklahoma Sooners played 49 players in their blowout victory over unranked TCU and the Tigers played 84 in their blowout win over the No. 15 N.C. State Wolfpack.

"Every year your roster is different. This year our roster is full of guys we trust, guys who deserve to play. I believe you play the guys who deserve to play," Swinney said. "We have a few dynamic freshmen who have emerged, guys who deserve to play. So we play them. We have the best running back in the country, but we're going to play those other guys, too. That helps him. That helps the morale of your team.

"Now, you don't play guys to play guys. Everyone has to be able to contribute. The confidence that grows in your team, the selflessness that grows in your team, that becomes beneficial. Now, I've had teams that the drop-off was so big from starters to backups that we couldn't be as free in terms of subbing. This particular roster is different. We have guys all over the field that we trust."

The Tigers will likely not be able to empty their bench this week against a Seminole team that is looking for their first marquee win of the Taggart-era.

But regardless of how many players play for the Tigers, Swinney is excited to try to pick up back-to-back victories in Tallahassee for the first time in school history.

"Our focus is to have another great week of preparation and try to build on the momentum that we have created. We have a lot of confidence right now. We have a lot of improving to do. I like the progress we have seen. I like where we are. We are also trying to figure some things out. I'm excited about it.

Wilkins making the most of senior season

The tendency in recent years for college athletes has been to take the proverbial money and run when it comes to turning professional or returning to school.

But for Clemson defensive end Christian Wilkins, the decision to return for his senior season has turned out to be one of the best decisions of his life.

"I just feel like this is definitely the closest team we've had," Wilkins said. "I've been around a long time, so I'm confident with certain things and aware of certain things. I just know what to expect, and it's fun to watch the young guys. I see their struggles and help them through that. Me being the older guy, I've gone through the same things and can help them with that. It's been great. I just try and be the best I can be for my teammates, and it makes it more fun and a lot easier."

When Wilkins announced in January that he would be returning to the Tiger program for his senior season, many around the country were left scratching their heads at the decision.

What could make a player decide to forego potentially millions of dollars? Why would a player risk career-ending injuries to play college football? Those questions, however, have answers—he loves college football.

"He's been so intentional in everything. He has enjoyed the entire journey, even mat drills," Clemson head coach Dabo Swinney said. "He has been so committed in what he came back to do. He loves his teammates. He graduated last December. You don't decide to do what he did unless you love it. He knows this is it. Last year this time he was torn. Now he knows this is it. In the spring game he played some safety and was having a ball. He is a great teammate and one of the best leaders we've ever been around. He's taken great care of his body. He's just enjoyed it all.

"He was with us last week handing out pizzas over at the (homecoming) floats. He's trying to finish strong. He takes pride in his role as a leader. He will show up today and will be excited for Tuesday's practice. That's who he is."

While Wilkins is making the most of his final season in a Tiger uniform, he also enjoys seeing some of the backups make the most of their time on the field this season—like fellow senior and former Orangeburg-Wilkinson standout Albert Huggins.

"It's fun to see Albert, someone I came in with (playing so well)," Wilkins said. "He's had a lot of ups and downs with his career, but it's good to see him be a consistent solid and dependable player."

Wilkins and Huggins are part of a senior class that is attempting to make history this week when the Tigers take on the Florida State Seminoles Saturday—

becoming the first senior class to finish their career with a 4-0 record against the Seminoles.

But as big of an accomplishment as that would be for Wilkins and the rest of the senior class, he is not worried about getting that record, just making sure that his squad is ready for the challenge.

"It will definitely be just another great accomplishment for the senior class," Wilkins said. "I feel like each year, the senior class is breaking some record or doing something that's never been done before. That will be a great accomplishment of course, but we are not necessarily focused on that. We are just focusing on coming to this FSU game prepared, so we can get that result.

"They've looked better definitely these past couple of weeks. They've been getting a couple of wins, a big win last week. It seems like they've started to put it together a little bit, so I'm definitely looking forward to the challenge."

The Game

The No. 2 Clemson Tigers (8-0, 5-0 ACC) used a dominant defensive performance and an explosive offensive to hand the Florida State Seminoles (4-4, 2-4 ACC) their worst home loss in school-history Saturday by a final score of 59-10 at Doak Campbell Stadium.

"Unbelievable day. I've been in a lot of really sad locker rooms coming down here, but an unbelievable day," Clemson head coach Dabo Swinney said. "I think this is three games in a row that we've played complete games and we're really just starting to get in a rhythm."

The Tigers' defense held the Seminoles offense to only 247 total yards (268 passing and -21 rushing), while the Tiger offense amassed 524 total yards (404 passing and 120 rushing).

"I thought our defense set the tempo for the day coming out...it took us about a quarter to settle in, but I thought int the second quarter we kind of took off," Swinney said. "Defensively we were awesome—five sacks and offensively that was the most points ever scored here (at Doak Campbell Stadium)...ever.'

After both teams got off to slow starts, as they combined for seven punts in the first quarter, it was the Tigers that opened the scoring.

The Tigers took over at their own 31-yard line and on the second play of the drive the offense finally got the spark they were looking for, as Trevor Lawrence (20-37 for 314 yards and three touchdowns) connected with Tee Higgins for a 41-yard gain. Six plays later, Lawrence once again found Higgins, this time for a 7-yard touchdown pass that capped an eight-play, 69-yard drive for the Tigers.

The Tigers continued to dominate the first half on next possession, as Lawrence once again found Higgins for their second touchdown of the first half that gave the Tigers a 14-0 lead. On the touchdown pass, Lawrence tied the freshman-record for touch- down passes (14) at Clemson—held by former Tiger quarterback Deshaun Watson.

The Seminoles had their best drive of the day going, as they reached the Clemson 40- yard line, but the Tiger defense ended the drive. On third-and-20, Deondre Francois' pass was intercepted by linebacker Tre Lamar —who returned the interception 43 yards to the Seminole 30-yard line.

Lawrence led the offense to the Seminole 1-yard line, before the Tigers turned to their "Jumbo Package" to finish off the drive—the package featured defensive linemen Christian Wilkins and Dexter Lawrence lined up in the I-formation—as Wilkins took the handoff from Lawrence and leapt into the end zone for his third career touchdown, first rushing, that extended the lead to 21-0.

Following the Seminoles sixth punt of the day, the Tigers needed on six-plays and 1:41 to go 73 yards and add a final touchdown of the first half—as tight end Garrett Williams' 2-yard rush gave the Tigers a 28-0 lead.

The Tigers continued their onslaught in the second half. After Derion Kendrick returned the opening kickoff 28 yards, the Tigers needed only two plays, including a 58-yard touchdown pass from Lawrence to Amari Rodgers, to extend the lead to 35-0. With his third touchdown pass of the day, Lawrence broke Deshaun Watson's fresh- man record for touchdown passes in a season (16).

"We had this guy named Deshaun Watson who was pretty special, but Trevor goes out there and breaks two records—just kind of ho-hum," Swinney said.

The Seminoles finally forced a Tiger punt on their second drive of the half, but Will Spiers' punt was muffed by D.J. Matthews and recovered by the Tigers at the Seminole 10-yard line.

However, the Tigers were forced to settle for a field goal by true freshman B.T. Potter that extended the lead to 38-0.

Lawrence extended his lead on the record for touchdown passes by a freshman on the next series, as he found Rodgers for the second time—this time it was a 68-yard connection that ended a one-play drive.

The Seminoles finally broke through, as a field goal by Ricky Aguayo capped a 10-play, 75-yard drive that cut the lead to 45-3.

The Tigers answered on their next series, as backup quarterback Chase Brice connected with Diondre Overton for a 61-yard pass to the Seminole 11-yard line. Three plays later Brice found T.J. Chase for a 5-yard touchdown pass that extended the lead to 52-3.

The Tigers continued to add to their lead following a Seminole punt that traveled 18 yards, as they needed only four plays before Adam Choice found the end zone from 15 yards out.

The Seminoles found the end zone for the first time in the game with 4:43 to play in the fourth quarter, as backup quarterback Sam Blackman connected with Keyshawn Helton for a 73-yard touchdown pass that cut the Tiger lead to 59-10.

Tiger Tracks:

Clemson has outscored opponents by 108 points in second quarters this season, the Tigers' largest point differential in any frame.

With Tre Lamar's interception, the Tigers have forced at least one takeaway in the last 16 games—the program's longest streak since an 18-game stretch spanning the 2004 & 2005 seasons.

Clemson has held five of their eight opponents scoreless in the first half. Opponents have scored a total of just 26 points on the Tigers in first halves this season.

Clemson played all 72 players that traveled for the third road game in a row.

Coaches Corner:

Dabo Swinney on Christian Wilkins becoming the first Clemson defensive lineman to score a rushing touchdown:

"Christian Wilkins in our 'Fridge Package' was able to get into the end zone... That guy is so greedy. He wants the ball. He wants to play kick returner, wide-out, quarterback

GAME 9: LOUISVILLE

While the offense has been heating up for the second-ranked Clemson Tigers (8-0, 5-0 ACC) over the last three games, which has seen the Tigers amass 163 points—an average of 54.3 points per game—it has been the Tigers' defense that has stepped up their play.

Over the same three game span, the Tiger defense has allowed only 20 total points—an average of 6.6 points per game. However, the defense may have not had a bigger impact on the outcome a game than they did in Saturday's 59-10 beatdown of the Florida State Seminoles because the offense struggled in the first quarter to find their groove.

"Thought our defense set the tempo for the day right out of the gate. We missed a couple plays early offensively," Clemson head coach Dabo Swinney said. "We had a touchdown, but overthrew it. I thought the second quarter we took off.

"Defensively, five sacks. Negative 21 yards rushing. We wanted to make them one-dimensional and take the run away and we were able to do that. That led us to being able to pin our ears back and disrupt the quarterback and the timing."

The Seminoles entered Saturday's game, ranked 93rd in the nation in scoring offense (25 points per game), 33rd in passing offense (265.7 yards per game) and 125th in rushing offense (98.43 yards per game).

While none of their statistics strike a great deal of fear into the hearts of opposing defenses, the fact is there was still a lot of very talented players on the offensive side of the ball—which made the defenses' performance that much more impressive.

"They've got a terrific group of skilled athletes, starting with the quarterback," Clemson defensive coordinator Brent Venables said earlier this week. "That's a terrific player and great quarterback and the running back, the skill at receiver and tight end...very, very talented group of players."

However, the Tiger defense was ready for the playmakers that the Seminoles ran onto the field. In fact, they held the Seminole offense to only 247 total yards of offense—including 268 yards passing and -21 yards rushing.

And even though that kind of dominant performance may have been a surprise to those watching the game, Venables sensed that his unit was ready for the challenge.

"I loved it. Great attitude. Business-like approach," Venables said. "Had a great week of practice. Woke up this morning and our guys were focused. Got a real hunger to them. They had the right stuff to them.

"Good leverage and positioning on the back end. Thought we had good cohesion between the front and back-end guys. They had some new wrinkles and I thought our guys made pretty good adjustments when the game was still in doubt."

With their defensive performance Saturday, the Tigers moved to third in the nation in total defense (allowing only 263.9 yards per game), to seventh in rush defense (91.63 yards per game) and to No. 1 in scoring defense (allowing only 13 points per game).

However, maybe more impressive than the incredible numbers the Tigers are putting up—both defensively and offensive—is the number of players they are doing it with. For the third-straight road game, the Tigers played all 72 players that traveled to the game—which is not only good for the team, but for the players as well.

"Obviously, I think from a morale standpoint, guys that have to work every bit as hard, have to show up every day, there is nothing that is more rewarding than the opportunity to play," Venables said. "That's why you work, and a lot of teams around the country don't reward that opportunity or create that opportunity for their guys like we have.

"Obviously, it builds depth and, whether it's injury or just continuing to develop your players, that's how you get better and there is not a better way to improve than to play."

Lawrence keeps winning over teammates

How does a true freshman enter one of the premier football programs in the nation and win over his teammates—he goes to work.

At least that is what true freshman quarterback Trevor Lawrence did in not only winning the starting job for the second-ranked Clemson Tigers, but also in winning over his teammates.

"Well he has just come in and gone to work. He has just gone to work every day." Clemson head coach Dabo Swinney said. "If you go back to January he came in and got in line and he has earned everything he has gotten. He has put the work in mentally and physically. And then you get to the season and he has gone and had the performance to match the work.

"He has done a great job. He is a special player obviously. He is very humble. He just goes about his business in a very humble way. He is a great teammate. He is a great winner. He has done a good job making good decisions and taking care of the ball. He has a very, very good understanding of our system but also what is happening on the defensive side. He is a playmaker so I am really proud of him."

But even coming in a "going to work" may not be enough to win over the veterans on the team—especially when you have an established quarterback like the Tigers had.

In fact, they had more than one quarterback on their roster that had waited his time. The Tigers entered this season with incumbent quarterback Kelly Bryant on the roster—who had just led the Tigers to a 12-2 season, a third-straight ACC championship and a third-straight appearance in the College Football Playoff, as well as backup quarterback Zerrick Cooper and Hunter Johnson—both of whom had played at different points in the 2017 season.

But as Lawrence rose up the depth chart, the other quarterbacks fell away—each of the three choosing to transfer—Cooper is currently the starting quarterback at Jacksonville State, Johnson has transferred to Northwestern and Bryant is currently looking into possible locations to play next season.

However, Swinney stated that it did not take long for his teammates to realize he was the real-deal.

"When these guys (freshmen) comes in all these veteran guys they watch everything they can from them," Swinney said. "He is a very quiet guy. He has just great respect for the veterans. How do these guys work? How do they practice? How do they handle adversity? He has just stayed poised and focused. But at the end of the day we always say game knows game. I think they all quickly realized that this guy can play.

"Then you throw in the fact that he is an easy guy to like because of how he handles himself. He is just a very unassuming guy. He is a very humble leader. He just doesn't expect anything more than anyone else. He lead by example. He's a worker. I think he earned the respect of everyone just by being who he has always been."

But don't let his "unassuming" nature fool you, because Lawrence is a winner and is not used to losing—as was demonstrated when a Florida State player was ejected last Saturday for a targeting penalty on Lawrence.

"Yeah you saw it. The play was over and (the Florida State player) was going to get (the ball). It got a little feisty afterwards," Swinney said. 'You are not a winner like Trevor if you don't have competitive fire to you. Don't mistake his Cool-Hand- Lukeness to him not having a blazing fire of competitiveness in his gut. He's a big-time winner and has got a great spirit to him. He just channels everything towards things that matter and help him win."

It is that kind of fight that has the Tigers rallying around their new leader this season.

"They know the character that he has. That he's not going to be a guy out there that's talking trash. He's going to let his play do the talking," co-offensive coordinator Tony Elliott said. "It was good to see our offensive line - I think John Simpson was the first one to run over to him. Everybody is jumping up. They appreciate who he is and know he doesn't play the game like that. They respect his work so they want to defend him. The first thing we talk about before we get on the bus on Saturdays to go to the game is 'Protect the quarterback. At all costs.' That's the guy that we got to take care of."

Tigers on the ROY bus

When the Clemson Tigers were announced as the No. 2 team in the first ranking by the College Football Playoff committee Tuesday night, head coach Dabo Swinney was not surprised by the Tigers being behind No.1 Alabama—even though the Tigers resume should have them at No.1

In fact, it is really not that close. The Alabama Crimson Tide have been dominant, but against a lesser schedule than the one the Tigers have played.

The Crimson Tide have just two wins against teams with a winning record and only one against a Top 25 team—Texas A&M. The Tigers have three wins against Top 25 teams—No. 19 Syracuse, No. 20 Texas A&M and No. 21 N.C. State. But Swinney is not worrying about those facts—yet. Instead he is just glad to be on the bus heading in the direction of the playoffs.

"The reality of it is, back when I was a player we kind of had the big-time bus and then the R.O.Y. bus – the Rest of Y'all – it is kind of Alabama and the rest of Y'all," Swinney said during an interview with ESPN's Rece Davis following the release of the rankings. "We are just kind of glad to be on the R.O.Y bus right now and to still have a chance. But, it really does not matter. It is exciting to know that we are getting into November and we are still a team that is in the middle of the hunt.

"The race is not over. You have to keep running the race with purpose and focus and great attention to the task at hand and just take them one at a time. Hopefully, when it is all said and done and Y'all get to about that fifth or however many shows that Y'all do, we are still in there, that would be awesome. For us, we want to win our division first. That is what we want to do."

The Game

The No. 2 Clemson Tigers (9-0, 6-0 ACC) continued their run of dominant play Saturday, as they cruised to a 77-16 victory over the Louisville Cardinals (2-7, 0-6 ACC) inside Death Valley.

The Tigers have outscored their last four opponents 240-36.

"I want to thanks the leadership we have in place," Clemson head coach Dabo Swinney said. "Those guys are incredible. Definitely a great start to Novembers. Our guys continue to do things that haven't been done or haven't been done in a long time."

The Tigers exploited the Cardinals' run defense, which entered the game ranked 125th in the nation, to the tune of 492 yards by five running backs—including three that finished the game with over 100 yards.

"I think this was the seventh time in school history that it's happened (having three players finish with 100 yards), and it's the third time this season—so, really proud of them," co-offensive coordinator Jeff Scott said.

In the game, the Tigers' scored at least 70 points against an ACC opponent for the second time in school history. They scored 82 points vs Wake Forest in 1981.

"We broke the record for most points in four straight games," Swinney said. "That record was in 1900 to some guy named (John) Heisman. Man they must have been carving teams up back then."

The Tigers wasted little time jumping on-top of the Cardinals, as they needed only four plays to go 75 yards in 1:15—culminated on a 10-yard touchdown run by Travis Etienne, who amassed 45 yards on two carries on the Tigers' opening drive.

After a three-and-out, the Tigers went back to work. This time they needed only one-play, a 70-yard touchdown run by Tavien Feaster, that extended the Tigers lead to 14-0.

The Cardinals finally found their offensive groove on their second drive of the day, as they started on their own 19-yard line and drove the ball to the Tigers' 16-yard line. The drive stalled after the Tiger defense held the Cardinals on third down and they settled for a 25-yard field goal by Blanton Creque that cut the Tigers' lead to 14-3.

On their ensuing drive, the Tigers continued their dominance, as Lawrence found Tee Higgins for an 11-yard touchdown that capped off an eight-play, 75-yard drive that extended the lead to 21-3.

The Tigers added to their lead on the next possession by the Cardinals, as Tiger safety Isaiah Simmons intercepted quarterback Jawon Pass' pass, the first career interception by Simmons, and returned it 27 yards for a touchdown.

After both teams struggled for the majority of the second quarter, the Tigers got back on the scoreboard. Quarterback Trevor Lawrence led the Tigers on a seven-play, 60-yard touchdown drive. The drive ended when Lawrence found Amari Rodgers from 3 yards out for his second passing touchdown of the day and gave the Tigers a 35-3 lead.

The Tigers took their opening possession and drove to the Cardinals' 2-yard line before they brought in their "Fridge package"—that debuted last week and featured defensive tackles Christian Wilkins and Dexter Lawrence in the I-formation. Last week, it was Wilkins who got his first career rushing touchdown. This week, it was Lawrence who took the handoff and found the end zone for his first career touchdown.

The Cardinals next possession lasted only one-play, as Pass threw his second interception of the day—this one to safety Tanner Muse, who returned the interception to the Cardinals' nine-yard line. The Tigers needed only three plays to add to their lead, as Feaster scored his second touchdown of the day.

Following the Cardinals fifth punt of the day, the Tigers took over at the Cardinals' 47-yard line and, behind backup quarterback Chase Brice, found the end zone for the eighth time—as Brice found Trevion Thompson in the end zone for a 6-yard touch- down.

The Cardinals appeared to have a little bit of life on the Tigers' next possession, as Brice fumbled the snap and it was recovered by the Cardinals, who then fumbled the ball back to the Tigers.

The Tigers took the good fortune and once again turned it into points, as they needed only two plays to cover the 74 yards. Brice found Justyn Ross for a 60-yard touchdown pass that capped the drive and extended the lead to 63-3.

On the ensuing kickoff the Cardinals found the end zone for the first time, as Hassan Hall returned the kickoff 93 yards for their first touchdown of the day. The extra point was blocked by Wilkins.

The Tigers answered the Cardinal touchdown on their next possession, as true freshman running back Lyn-J Dixon broke free for a 55-yard touchdown run that extended the lead to 70-9. However, the Cardinals found the end zone for the second time of the day on their next possession on a 10-yard rush by Mal Cunningham.

The Tigers' continued their barrage in a special way, as head coach Dabo Swinney's son Will became the 10th Tiger to score a touchdown on Brice's third touchdown pass of the game.

"I was happy for him," Swinney said. "The biggest thing is seeing his teammates get- ting excited for him. I'm proud of him, as a dad I'm really happy for him."

Tiger Tracks

Tee Higgins became the first Clemson player to catch a touchdown in four straight games since former Lake Marion Gator and current Los Angelas Charger Mike Williams posted two four-game streaks in 2016.

Clemson rushed for 158 yards in the first quarter, its third-most in any quarter in the past 15 seasons

Clemson offensive lineman Mitch Hyatt broke the Clemson record for the most snaps played in school history.

Coaches Corner

Co-offensive coordinator Jeff Scott on the offensive output in recent week:

"We talked about, offensively, that we had another step to take and we felt that we did that today."

Player Perspective

The Tigers are two-for-two when utilizing their newfound "Fridge package." However, when asked about whether or not anyone has been able to stop the unique package in practice, Dexter Lawrence had a short answer, "Come on bro."

GAME 10: BC

"When Coach Swinney took over, he wanted to bring some uniformity to our uniform policy," co-offensive coordinator Jeff Scott said. "In the past, it was seniors get to vote what they want to wear...and Coach Swinney wanted there to be some consistency. I think from the beginning, he started that we only wear those orange pants when there's a championship on the line. So, I think our guys know that we've got an opportunity to win the division championship this week and that means we get to put those orange pants on and it's something that they look forward too and take a lot of pride in."

Those championship pants will come with a great challenge this week, as the Tigers will take on a Boston College team that is in the midst of one of their best seasons in recent history, and are also in control of their own destiny in the division race.

"We've got a great challenge and great opportunity this week in Boston College," Scott said. "Obviously, it's an opportunity for us to accomplish our second goal which is to win the division. The way our goals are set up...the first goal is to win the opener and then it's taken us 10 weeks now to get an opportunity to reach our second goal-- which is win the division. We've been racking off a lot of different records and things that haven't been done--I don't believe there's been an ACC team win four division trophies since they started the two divisions. So, that will be something our guys have an opportunity to accomplish."

While the Eagles defense has yet to face an offense with the fire-power of the Tigers this season, there is an understanding that they will have to play one of their best games of the season.

"Have a lot of respect for Boston College. They are very, very consistent," Scott said. "You know exactly what you're going to get with them. Very well coached, disciplined, very physical, hard-nosed team and defense. They're going to make you earn everything that you get--there's not gimmies with their defense. There never has been. I think that they're playing very confident on defense and I think they're very experienced. They've got nine starters coming back from last year's defense and eight of the 11 starters on defense are all juniors or seniors.

"They are fourth in the country in interceptions, they are fifth in the country in caused turnovers, they are 12th in the country in red-zone defense--then their defensive end, No. 11, Ray is fifth in the country in sacks."

Even with the cold weather and a fanbase that is primed for an upset with Game- Day on campus for only the third time in the school's history, the Tigers are excited about the challenge before them.

"It will be a great challenge and like we tell our guys, when you are trying to accomplish something special and have a chance to win championships...it's not going to be easy," Scott said. "It's difficult. If it was easy, then there would be a lot more people doing it. So, it will be a great challenge, but I know our guys are excited about it and looking forward to it."

Carving up opponents

The second-ranked Clemson Tigers appear to be preparing for Thanksgiving later this month, as they continue to carve up opponents in historic fashion following Saturday's 77-16 victory over the Louisville Cardinals.

The Tigers have outscored its last four opponents (all ACC opponents) by a margin of 240-36. Clemson's differential of 204 points is the largest in four consecutive ACC contests in conference history, surpassing Florida State's margin of 184 points in 2000.

And with 240 points in the last four games, Clemson broke the previous team record for points in a four-game span, set in 1900 (208). That four-game stretch in 1900 featured point totals of 39, 12 and 35 prior to a 122-0 win vs. Guilford.

"This week we told our guys, even though we've played well the last few weeks there's still another step we could take," Scott said. "I think we averaged 13.3 yards per rush which is a Clemson record. Having three backs over a hundred yards was awesome to see, and we had 10 different guys score a touchdown. Nine of those guys were on offense and Isaiah had the pick-six. It's nice being able to score a lot of different ways.

"The last four games I believe we've scored more points in the history of the school over a four-game stretch. I'm really proud of how we're playing and our goal this time of year is to continue to improve and get better each week as we begin this championship phase and I think we did that today."

In fact, the 77 points in Saturday's were the fourth-most in a game in program history, trailing only contests against Guilford (122-0 on Oct. 5, 1901), Furman (99-0 on Sept. 25, 1915) and Wake Forest (82-24 on Oct. 31, 1981).

The Tigers reached the 70-point mark against an ACC opponent for only the second time in program history, joining the school's 82-point output against Wake Forest on Oct. 31, 1981. It marks the sixth time in ACC history that a team has scored 70 points in a conference game.

But more important points scored, is the way in which the Tigers are scoring points.

The two weeks prior to Saturday's game featured an all-out air assault led by true freshman quarterback Trevor Lawrence—in which he threw for more than 600 yards and had seven touchdowns in the two games. Saturday's blowout win featured a return to the ground attack.

For the second time this season, the Tigers set a school record in yards per carry. The Tigers rushed for 13.3 yards per carry, surpassing the program record of 11.8, set earlier this season at Wake Forest.

They also rushed for 492 yards, its most under Dabo Swinney and the fourth- most in team history—and had three backs rush for more than 100 yards, it marked the seventh time in team history and second time this season that the Tigers had three different players rush for 100 yards in a single game. It also marks the first time the Tigers have accomplished the feat twice in one year.

"I remember the days when we struggled to get one guy over 100 yards, something that we take for granted now," Scott said. "This isn't a selfish group. It's very selfless and those guys work every week."

Even though the Tigers' offense appears to be running with flawless ease right now, the scary thing for opposing defenses is that they believe they can still get better.

"Ten different guys scored touchdowns for us, and we had over 600 yards of offense. We also had three running backs go for over 100 yards," head coach Dabo Swinney said. "We had a season-high six sacks, and that was our 17th game in a row with a pick. That was a great interception by Isaiah Simmons. It was fun to see so many guys getting an opportunity to play. Over 90 guys played for us. Dexter Lawrence even got himself a touchdown.

"That was a good experience for our team, and it was a lot of fun. We're 9-0, but we're not satisfied. We want to win our division, and we'll have that opportunity next week. We've worked all year to get to this point, so we'll enjoy this win and get back to work on Monday."

The Game

On a frigid night at No. 17 Boston College (7-3, 4-2 ACC) the No. 2 Clemson Tigers (10-0, 7-0 ACC) punched their ticket to the ACC Championship Saturday night, as they clinched their fourth straight ACC Atlantic Division title in front of a sell out crowed of 44,500 by a final score of 27-7.

"Just a tough hard-fought game—knew it would be coming up here," Clemson head coach Dabo Swinney said. "They're a huge challenge. Just really proud of our guys coming up here.

Just really proud of our guys for what they've accomplished and made history tonight (becoming the first ACC team to win four straight division titles)...Really cool to get the division win here—and I'm thankful to our fans who get to go back to Charlotte for a fourth straight time."

The Tigers used a stingy defense that held the Eagles to only 113 total yards (104 passing and nine rushing) and an impressive passing performance from quarterback Trevor Lawrence (29-40 for 295 yards, one touchdown and one interception) to continue their dominant run in the ACC.

"I am really proud of Trevor to come up here and really lead us," Swinney said. "This was a big-time game for him..Defensively our guys were really dialed in...and our guys did an awesome job."

They have outscored their last five opponents 267-43.

The Tigers opened the scoring on their first drive of the game. They needed only only three plays before they found their way into Eagle territory, as Lawrence found a wide-open Amari Rodgers for a 41-yard gain to the Eagles 18-yard line. The Tigers reached the 12-yard line before they settled for a 30-yard field goal from Greg Huegel that put them on top 3-0.

The Eagles answered the Tigers score without running an offensive play, as the Tigers' punt from Will Spiers was returned 74 yards for a touchdown that gave the Eagles a 7-3 lead.

The Tigers responded on their next drive behind the arm of Lawrence. The Tigers took the ball from their own 30-yard line and proceeded to the Eagles 2-yard line where the Tigers faced a fourth-and-goal from the 2-yard line. The Tigers ran a wrinkle from their "Fridge package", as Lawrence faked the ball to the defensive tackle Christian Wilkins and found a wide-open Milan Richard for the touchdown.

"Christian really wanted the ball, but I told him, 'No, this is going to be wide- open—and it was," Swinney said.

After the Eagles starting quarterback Anthony Brown was knocked out of the game on their first series, the Tigers forced a three-and-out on their second series of the game. Following the punt the Tigers added to their lead, as Huegel connected on his second field goal of the game that capped off an eight-play, 56-yard drive.

After both teams managed only a field goal in the second quarter, the Tigers got rolling in the second half.

After forcing the sixth punt of the night on the Eagles first possession of the second half, the Tigers needed only three plays to go 64 yards and a 6-yard touchdown run by Lawrence to extend the lead to 20-7.

The Tigers answered the Eagles earlier touchdown with a punt return for a touch- down, as Rodgers took the ninth punt of the night 58 yard for his first career punt return touchdown that extended the lead to 27-7.

Player Perspective

Christian Wilkins on what it means to clinch the division one hour from his home:

"Definitely it was special to me to come here an hour from my home and do something, along with the other seniors, that had never been done before (four straight titles)."

Tiger Tracks

Travis Etienne crossed the 1000-yard mark on just his 117th carry of the season.

Hunter Renfrow tied former Tiger Artavis Scott for the school record with 38 straight games with a reception.

Trevor Lawrence passed Deshaun Watson for the most yards of total offense by a true freshman in school history.

Clelin Ferrell moved alone into 5th in Clemson history with his 24th career sack, breaking a tie with Keith Adams and Adrian Dingle.

GAME 11: DUKE

True freshman quarterback Trevor Lawrence was supposed to struggle with the cold temperatures that he was going to face when the second-ranked Clemson Tigers traveled north to Boston College.

"I think (the weather) should affect him somewhat. We are going to get a chance to see it. No one knows, right? He's never played in this type of weather," Desmond Howard told the media Friday. "I think the offensive coordinators, they're going to have to try and figure out if the wind's in their face, if the wind's at their back, are they going to take a shot downfield. All those things are going to play into the game plan tomorrow night."

Howard double-down on his questioning of Lawrence and the weather during Saturday's broadcast of ESPN's College Gameday.

"I've played in some very cold places before and I know this affects a team from a warm weather area," Howard said. "I think because of the talent that Clemson has -

these guys are going to come out and play of control, but when the weather smacks them in the face - it's a difference-maker. Boston College will upset Clemson."

But contrary to the analyst's opinion, the weather did not effect Lawrence—in fact, he threw for 295 yards and one touchdown, and added his first career rushing touchdown,

"We put up over 400 yards. Tough yards that you have to earn," Clemson head coach Dabo Swinney said. "Really proud of Trevor Lawrence. This is a tough environment and he came up here and led us. A few misses and a few mistakes. He cost us some points maybe on that third down (sliding). But he's continuing to get better and grow every week. This was a big time game for him."

Lawrence also was named the recipient of the Leather Helmet Award as the game's most valuable player as awarded by the Boston College Gridiron Club.

"It's really cool. I mean, we talked about it last week because Travis (Etienne) won it last year," Lawrence said. "But really it's cool to win it. I felt like we played well, played tough. Obviously, it was cold out there and they had a good team. So it was cool to go out and play well."

When asked whether or not he was nervous about taking Lawrence into a hostile, cold environment in prime time with a division title on the line, Swinney said that there was only one thing he was concerned with—whether or not his team would re- member how to play the game.

"Listening to all the reports out there, I kind of thought we might forget how to play football," Swinney said. "That was the only thing I was worried about, that we were gonna freeze up and not be able to tackle and run.

I was kind of disappointed it was only a balmy 38 out there.

"That's the only thing that I was nervous about was that we were going to freeze up and forget how to run and tackle."

Lawrence and the Tigers better be glad they proved they can play in cold weather because the low temperature next Saturday night is supposed to be 31 when the Tigers take on the Duke Blue Devils.

"It's just football. We gotta come out a play. The weather's not going to win a game," Lawrence said. "Obviously they were more used to it than us, but at the end of the day it's just football."

Williams honored to play at Clemson

For many college athletes, the idea of leaving school early is a decision that is made due to a need for money, a desire to move onto the next level of play—whether it be the NFL, the NBA, MLB or PGA Tour.

But for one Tiger the decision whether or not to return for a final season of football has nothing to do with any of those desires. In fact, it is a much nobler desire—to serve his country.

"My grandfathers both served, one was in the Navy, and one was in the Marine Corps," tight end Garrett Williams said. "I've had the opportunity to meet a number of Marine Corps veterans through Clemson football and also through my dad. At this time, I want to go into the Marine Corps and if I could be an infantry officer in the Marine Corps that would be an awesome career and honor to serve."

The decision is one that he has struggled with ever since redshirting last season after suffering a torn ACL.

"It's something I've been thinking about for a while. I came in here and didn't redshirt originally. I played my first two years and tore my ACL so I sat out my third year, so in a sense, I've always felt like a senior," Williams said. "I'm thankful for the opportunity to potentially play another year but right now I'm just going back and forth on what I want to do.

Even though he still has one year of eligibility left, for head coach Dabo Swinney, the honor of being recognized on Senior Day is something that is reserved for those who have put in the work academically and not on the basis of having expired their eligibility.

"We don't run juniors down the hill. You have to be a senior (academically)," Swinney said. "Deshaun and Mike Williams were graduates that coming December. We do it based on academics, not eligibility. Christian wasn't sure what he was going to do but he was graduating in December, so we honored him. He might be my first guy who's been honored twice. It's like a two-time curtain call for Christian."

It is that reason—Williams will graduate in December—that Swinney insisted that he be honored with his fellow Tigers who will be honored Saturday. And it is that kind of insistence that makes Swinney and the Clemson program so special for him.

"At this point, I'm not 100-percent sure on what I want to do," Williams said. "But after talking with Coach (Dabo) Swinney, he told me that even if it was a consideration of mine to leave that he wanted to give me the opportunity to walk on senior day and experience that just in case.

"I'm thankful for that and it just shows you how great coach Swinney is honestly. He cares about us and wants us to experience everything. I love this place with all my heart and if I did make the decision to leave that would be very difficult to do. I'm go- ing to follow God's plan for me and listen to him."

For the future Marine, Military Appreciation Day at Clemson is always a special day and an honor to take part in the game that recognizes the Tigers' storied military history and also remembers those who paid the ultimate sacrifice.

"It's a tremendous honor to play in the game, I think that Clemson does it so well, I've never gotten to see all of the ceremonies but my parents talk about how great it is," Williams said. "It's such an honor to play in the game, I have so much admiration for the people who serve and have served and if we can honor them for just one game that's the least we could do.

Military Appreciation means more to Ross

Military Appreciation Day is always a special time at Clemson.

The Tigers' game against Duke was Clemson's 25th Military Appreciation Day. The history of the special day dates to 1994 when Clemson had a special flyover for the Clemson vs. Georgia Tech game on Nov. 12, just one day after Veteran's Day. Clemson had a flyover of four F-16s from Shaw Air Force Base during pregame as the highlight of the celebration that day.

Clemson has celebrated its military history every year since with the games held in November or when Clemson plays host to a school with its own military heritage.

Clemson has a 20-4 record in the previous 24 Military Appreciation Day games. The Tigers have won 10 such games in a row, with the last loss coming against Virginia Tech in 2007.

However, for some members of the Tigers' team the day is more than donning all-purple uniforms for the only time this season. For some players like true freshman wide receiver Justyn Ross, the game means more because his mom, Charay Franklin, has served overseas in the Navy and has been deployed as a part of the Alabama National Guard.

"Yes, she will be here. I mean, its military appreciation, I just want to dedicate this game to my mom. Just because of what she's done and what she's been through," Ross said. "Yeah, I'm excited about my first-night game, just being out there and seeing what the atmosphere is like at night time.

"I'm excited for my first night game (at Death Valley). Just being out there and seeing what the atmosphere is like in a night time."

Smith was unable to attend Clemson a year ago when Ross came for an official visit, as she was deployed. However, when she found out that the Tigers would be honoring the military for their game against The

Citadel, it was more important than even Ross understood at the time.

"Yeah, it did (have an impact on her). After the fact, she was telling me that it meant a lot to her because I took my official on Military Appreciation Day, so It does take a big toll on her," Ross said.

Now a part of the team, Ross believes that the family atmosphere and leadership of veterans like Hunter Renfrow have helped him succeed—as he has amassed 495 yards receiving (second on the team), five touchdowns and a team-high 19.8 yards per reception.

"The leadership that we have here. The family type culture, everybody in the locker room gets along. They know when and when not to do things. Just being around a good family," Ross said. "Now that I actually know him (Renfrow) and know who he is, it really does surprise me the things he can do. Renfrow can do almost anything, he plays quarterback sometimes, he punted the ball against wake forest for like 50 yards, so he can really do anything.

"I really wanted to meet him, to see who he was and how big he really was. Now that I actually see him it kind of surprises me what he's done over the past few years."

The Game

The second-ranked Clemson Tigers (11-0, 8-0 ACC) wrapped up a perfect ACC season Saturday night, as they defeated the Duke Blue Devils (7-4,3-4 ACC) by a final score of 35-6 in front of 81.500 purple-clad fans inside Death Valley.

"I'm really proud of our team. Obviously we did not get off to a good start. I was very disappointed in the start," Clemson head coach Dabo Swinney said. "Offensively we just couldn't get into any rhythm in the first half.

"I can't remember when we had as many drops. I was really disappointed in how we started but the good news is it is a four quarter game."

The Tigers won the first 11 games of a season for the second time under Head Coach Dabo Swinney (2015). Swinney would become the first coach in Clemson history to coach the school to multiple 11-0 starts, as legendary coaches Frank Howard and Danny Ford only accomplished the feat once each, in 1948 and 1981, respectively.

At the end of the day, they've been playing football at Clemson for a while and not many schools get to an 11-0 record," Swinney said.

The 2018 senior class became the first in league history to win 30 regular season conference games.

"They've won a bunch of ACC games," Swinney said. "Especially to win 11 in a row and all of the ACC games."

After both teams exchanged two punts, it was the Blue Devils that broke the scoreless tie. The Blue Devils started their drive at their own 2-yard line, but quickly made it to the Tiger 15-yard line behind the arm of quarterback Daniel Jones (24-43 for 158 yards, no touchdowns and no interceptions).

However, the Tiger defense held the Blue Devils to a 34-yard field goal that capped a 13-play, 83-yard drive.

After the Tigers third punt of the first quarter, the Blue Devils added to their lead when Collin Wareham connected on his second field goal of the day, a 32-yard kick, that extended the lead to 6-0.

On their next drive the Tigers finally woke up, as quarterback Trevor Lawrence (21-35 for 251 yards, two touchdowns and no interceptions) threw for 63 yards, including a 41-yard completion to Justyn Ross that led to a 2-yard touchdown run by Tavien Feaster.

After both teams exchanged a combined seven punts, the Tigers got back in the end zone. The Tigers needed only eight plays to go 68 yards, as Lawrence found Ross for a 19-yard touchdown that extended the lead to 14-6.

The Tigers struggled to find their running game in the first half, as they amassed only 17 yards on the ground, but got it going again on their opening drive of the second half. Travis Etienne (nine rushes for 81 yards and two touchdowns) gained 47 yards, including a 27-yard touchdown run that capped off a five-play, 61-yard drive and extended the lead to 21-6.

The Tigers continued to roll on their next possession. Following a missed field goal, the Tigers used the air and the ground to add to their lead. Lawrence found Derion Kendrick for a 33-yard gain on third-and-5, then immediately found T.J. Chase for a 9-yard gain before Etienne scored for the second time of the day from 29 yards out.

On the touchdown run, Etienne tied the Clemson single-season record for touchdowns with 17—held jointly by Lester Brown (1978), James Davis (2006) and Wayne Gallman (2016).

Following the eighth punt of the night for the Blue Devils, the Tigers added to their lead—as Lawrence found Chase in the end zone for a touchdown that capped off a 13- play drive and extended the lead 35-7.

Tiger Tracks:

Mitch Hyatt breaks the school record for the most starts in Clemson history

Hunter Renfrow just set the record for most consecutive games with a reception

More history for Hunter as he made his 43rd career start to break Terry Smith's school record for career starts by a wide receiver (42 from 1990-93).

Clelin Ferrell set a new career-high for sacks with 10.5—the first Tiger to reach double-digit sacks since Carlos Watkins in 2014.

Trevor Lawrence broke Kyle Parker's school record for touchdown passes by a freshman (20) and now has 21 touchdown passes on the year.

Coaches Corner:

Clemson offensive coordinator Jeff Scott on wide receiver Hunter Renfrow, who

left the game in the second quarter after suffering an injury.

"He still knew what day it was; He still knew what day he's getting married in April. I think he could have come back into the game, but (the trainers) wanted to hold him out for precautionary reasons."

GAME 12: SOUTH CAROLINA

Clemson head coach Dabo Swinney likes to say that every game is the biggest game of the season for his Tigers. While that may draw snickers and sneers from the fans and media for the first 11 games of the season, the 12th game is definitely the biggest one of the year—because it is South Carolina.

Whether you are a player or a coach, when week 13 finally rolls around, you know what it means.

"We are focused on winning the game," Elliott said. "This is something that is big for the state. It is personal for me. It is personal for a lot of guys from the state of South Carolina, and for the players that may not be from the state, it is going to be personal to them down the road."

While it is "personal" to the Gamecocks, who will be looking to end the Tigers' four- game winning streak and crush their hopes of making a fourth-straight appearance in the College Football Playoff, it is also very personal to the Tigers.

"Honestly, it's personal. It makes me want to focus more on a day-to-day basis whether I'm out at practice or from kick to kick mainly because I've got a lot of buddies that go there," former Blythewood High School kicker Greg Huegel said. "Say I miss a field goal or if it's a close game, no matter what, I'm going to hear about it at the end of the day. It's really just staying focused and getting the job done.

"I get a lot of people talking crap, but it is what it is."

For the Tiger true freshman duo of quarterback Trevor Lawrence and wide receiver Justyn Ross, this week will be their first induction into just how heated the rivalry gets between the two in-state schools.

"I'm not from here so I don't know a ton, but just watching it on TV when they were at South Carolina, I saw the hostility and the atmosphere and how the game went," Lawrence said. "Anyone who is watching can tell it's a pretty intense rivalry."

While Lawrence is relying the TV to get an idea of how intense the rivalry is, Ross is leaning on the knowledge of those who have played in the game—namely wide receivers Tee Higgins and Diondre Overton—to give him advise on the game.

While Lawrence has spent the majority of his senior season setting and breaking records, there is another thing that is equally as important to him—sending a second- straight senior class out with a perfect record against the Gamecocks.

"It's a big game. I'm just going to have a good week of preparation and get ready for it. It would mean a lot to me," Lawrence said. "The biggest thing is it's the next game. That's one of our goals to win every game we play against them. It's the next game but it's a big game because it's against South Carolina but it's another team that's in the way of what we're trying to do. It would mean a lot to help these seniors never lose to South Carolina. It would be awesome."

One of those seniors that is trying to leave with an undefeated record over the Gamecocks is defensive end Clelin Ferrell.

For the redshirt junior, after being a part of the game for four years, he understands just what this game means to the fans, the players and the coaches because, again, it's personal.

"I know it's kind of amplified for everyone else in this state. Obviously, this is the state championship," Ferrell said. "The fans are obviously not very fond of each other. It's a lot of history between us but we just want to treat it like another game. We know it's kind of personal and you want to go out against your so-called rival in the last game of the season. It's going to be a good game. They're a very good team and they have a lot of good players. We just have to go out and prepare. We have to have a great week of practice.

"Obviously, you want to be playing well when you go into the state championship. Obviously, we know it is going to be a tough hard-fought game, and because it is South Carolina it is going to be a bit personal. It's good to be kind of hitting our stride right when this game happens."

Mike Williams opens up about the rivalry

While many around the state of South Carolina are busy eating their turkey, the second-ranked Clemson Tigers will be thinking about chicken, as they preparing for their annual post-Thanksgiving matchup with the South Carolina Gamecocks.

While the Tigers and Gamecocks are gearing up for their game, former Clemson, Lake Marion Gator and current Los Angeles Charger Mike Williams will be watching the Tigers take on the Gamecocks from his home.

"For sure, I'm watching that," Williams told The T&D in an exclusive interview.

Williams did not hold back on his thoughts about the rivalry and his plans for a little extracurricular fun with former Gamecock defensive lineman Melvin Ingram, now his teammate.

"It's going to be a lot of trash talking," Williams said. "I don't think South Carolina good enough for him to bet me though. So, I think it might just be a whole lot of trash talking going on and maybe we'll just bet on whoever wins the other person has to wear the other teams shirt or something like that."

The Tigers have dominated the series with the Gamecocks, as they own a 69-4- 42 record against their rival—including having won the last four games in a row.

But for Williams, even though he had heard about the rivalry, he did not understand what it meant to the fans and the people of the state until he suited up for his first game against the Gamecocks.

"I didn't know until I actually played in a game, that's when I figured out that this right here is crazy," Williams said. "Fans really go crazy over this game and people be crying like over this game. That's when you realize this rivalry means so much for this state and a lot more than the people going out there playing and the coaches--this game really means a lot to the people also.

"Well, you hear about it before going and actually playing and you watch the games, but you don't know what it's really like until you actually out there on the field playing. All the emotions and everything that comes with the game is different--it's got a different vibe around campus and everybody just talks about it differently from home, because it's a rivalry game with both South Carolina teams. It just brings up a lot of different energy from the outsiders. You just have to focus and treat it as just another game."

Piggyback rides:

The last time that Williams suited up for a game against the Gamecocks was Nov. 26, 2016, a game that saw the Tigers beat the Gamecocks 56-7—the schools second-largest margin of victory over the Gamecocks (51-0 in 1900).

But the play that, now two years later, has been immortalized on t-shirts, bumper stickers and on social media came with 5:53 to play in the second quarter. With the Tigers leading 7-0, William caught a pass from former quarterback Deshaun Watson on the Gamecock 8-yard line and proceeded to give Gamecock defender Jamarcus King a piggyback ride into the end zone.

It was a play that Williams believes will live forever in the history of the rivalry.

"For sure, that's something that I feel like that's going to live forever when you talk about South Carolina and Clemson," Williams said. "We beat them pretty bad, so that game right there was like a game I'll always remember. I didn't want to lose to those guys, not once. Unfortunately, I lost to them my freshman year and then won the rest of them after that. So, we've just got to keep the streak going."

Turning around the hometown:

Williams understood when he committed to be a Clemson Tiger that he would hear about his decision to spurn the Gamecocks from those members of his hometown.

The Vance native, understood that the only way to quiet the naysayers was to go out and beat the Gamecocks—

which, except for his first year, was exactly what he and the Tigers did.

"For me, there was a lot of South Carolina fans where I was at, so I was kind of hearing it," Williams said. "So, when I came to Clemson I kind of changed a lot of those people--a lot of people were rooting for Clemson because of me. We kind of shut that up quick by winning. You know they had they five in a row--when I committed to Clemson that's all I was hearing was about the five in a row and this and that. But after we started winning, I feel like a lot more people down where I'm at started liking Clemson just because we beat them."

Turning the page:

Even though Williams has not been a part of the Tigers' program for the last two season, since turning professional following the 2016 season, he still keeps up with the Tigers.

And the Tigers recent run of success against the Gamecocks is not surprising because he understands the kind of players that head coach Dabo Swinney recruits.

"Yeah, for sure (I expected this), it was just being recruited to Clemson, we seen the guys coming in and we had a chance to be successful and a chance to go on a run for a while," Williams said. "That's just showing who Coach Swinney and the rest of the coaching staff, who they recruit, bring in the program and who they want to go out and have fun."

Williams chooses to not bother the current Tigers with phone calls and text messages because he remembers what it was like for him as a player.

"I haven't really been in contact with none of the players this year," Williams said. "I just kind of let players focus and do what they do to get through the season. I don't really like to blow people up. When I was in college, I just liked to go out there and play. I didn't really want anybody, good luck this, good luck that--just go out there and play. I know those guys are working hard and it's showing on the field. They are dominating during games. I just feel like they are going to be well-prepared for the game."

The thing that has impressed Williams this season is not the offensive numbers or the defensive prowess with which the Tigers are playing, instead it is the fact that everybody is contributing—which is a good sign for years to come.

"Everybody making plays. It's not just one person, you seeing just one person just going out there and you have to depend on that one person--it's a team effort," Williams said. "You see a lot of young players making plays and that just shows they going to be doing the same thing next year."

Williams played with arguably the greatest quarterback in Clemson football history, Deshaun Watson, and is currently playing with one of the best quarterbacks in the NFL, Phillip Rivers, so he knows what he is talking about when it comes to quarterbacks.

While he is not ready to say that true freshman quarterback Trevor Lawrence is on the same level as Watson—he is not far behind.

"As a freshman, I would probably say he can sling the ball pretty well," Williams said. "I feel like Deshaun was a better runner. He was a better runner probably, but they both have a strong arm, read defenses and will put the ball where it need to be."

The Tigers can beat the Tide:

For a player that faced the Alabama two times, and beat the Tide in his final game, the 2017 National Championship, Williams believes that should the Tigers and the Tide meet for a fourth straight season the Tigers will emerge victorious.

But his advise to the 2018 Tigers is to not worry about that game and focus on winning the next one.

"Oh yeah, take it one game at a time," Williams said. "Don't look ahead too fast because that's when you start to forget what you're working for. Just continue to focus on one game at a time and everything else will happen good."

Prediction for the Clemson-South Carolina game:

"It's in Death Valley. A night game. Oh my God," Williams said. "What was it last time? 56-7. I don't know they might go for like 70 this time. They might go for 70, for real. 'Cause it's like when they playing now, it's like, 'Well the backups in now and they ain't gonna score.' But the backup's going in and doing the same thing the starter is doing. Like, they don't miss a beat-- that's why they scoring so much. So, they might score about 70--probably. South Carolina might score about 10. If we score 70--I'll give them 10."

Swinney focused on the big-picture

"I think it's great to beat our rival. Yeah, okay, we beat them five times in a row-- well, great. Nobody's going to care next year," Swinney said. "You don't get to carry over any of the plays, you've got to go prove it every year. To me, that's a huge deal. I mean, there's been two 12-0 teams in the history of our school--'81 and '15...I mean. you go to any school, how many 12-0 teams have there been at any program. There's probably just a handful. That's hard. That's really hard to do."

To say that it has been hard to go undefeated in the regular season may be a massive understatement.

In fact, if the Tigers win this week it will be only the third time in school history they have accomplished that feat—joining the 1981 and 2015 teams. Swinney would also become the first Clemson coach in school history to have multiple 12-0 starts (2015), as Danny Ford accomplished the feat one during the 1981 season.

"Just look around college football there's what three, four undefeated teams, it's just hard to win week in and week out," Swinney said. "I have such a great respect for this team and how we've played from a totality standpoint in these previous 11 games. They have just had this incredible will to win, they've had this incredible will to prepare week in and week out. That would be an unbelievable accomplishment, in this day and age to go 12-0.

"Look around college football and all the parity and anybody can beat anybody on any given week and to have that type of consistency. We've played more teams, it's not like we've played The Village Idiot University, we've played the most teams in the country that have seven or more wins...Maybe the next team in the country has played four or five. So, that's impressive."

In 2013, after the Gamecocks won their fifth straight game over the Tigers, photos began to emerge of South Carolina fans, who had their picture taken with Swinney, holding up five fingers in the photo.

If the Tigers are able to finish off a 12-0 regular season, you will not see Swinney doing any "5-bombs" (holding up five fingers) because he will just be happy that his team finished off the regular season 12-0

"You won't see me doing in 5-bombs or any of that stuff if we were to win," Swinney said during his weekly press conference. "I'll just be happy that we won the game. I'm all about what's in front of us and what's after that.

"This is an exciting week. This is the season for us and then South Carolina. This is a goal of its own for us. It's important to everybody in this state. It's a lot of fun to be able to participate in rivalry games. It's something that's been woven into my life my entire 49 years. It's always a special week...I would love more than anything to see them be able to finish and to be one of those 12-0 teams that's rare in college football."

The Game

The No. 2 Clemson Tigers won their fifth straight game over the South Carolina Gamecocks and secured the seventh-perfect regular season in school history by a final score of 56-35 inside Death Valley Saturday night.

""I'm so proud of our team. It's so hard to go 12-0," Clemson head coach Dabo Swinney said. "It's only the third time ever that's been done here. Also, what an amazing accomplishment for this team to achieve something that hasn't been done in my lifetime by beating South Carolina five times in a row."

While many were expecting the Tiger offense to have little trouble moving the football against the Gamecock defense, few expected the Gamecocks to have a great deal of success against a Tiger defense that ranked first in scoring defense and third in total defense. But what ensued was a shootout, as both teams combined for 1,339 yards of offense (903 passing and 441 rushing) and 91 points.

"Give South Carolina credit for making plays and continuing to compete," Swinney said. "At the end of the day, our team was too strong across the board. I take my hat off to my players and staff to win a rivalry game by three touchdowns.

"That was an amazing performance by our offense. Trevor [Lawrence] was unbelievable in his first rivalry game. Our receivers made tons of plays. Hunter Renfrow made some amazing plays on third down. Our offense played maybe its best game of the season and had great balance. All of our running backs ran well, and our offensive line dominated and gave up no sacks."

The Gamecocks took the opening drive of the game and did what few teams this season have done to the Tiger defense—drove straight down the field. Behind the pass- ing of Jake Bentley (30-48 for 455 yards, five touchdowns and one interception), who completed six-of-eight passes for 65 yards on the drive, including a 9-yard touchdown pass to Deebo Samuel, the Gamecocks took the lead 7-0 over the Tigers.

The Tigers answered the Gamecock touchdown on their first possession, as Trevor Lawrence (27-36 for 393 yards, one touchdown and no interceptions) completed all four of his pass attempts for 57 yards before the Tigers turned to senior Adam Choice, who scored from 1-yard out and capped a 10-play, 75-yard drive that tied the game 7-7.

Following a 55-yard punt by the Gamecocks, the Tigers started their next drive at their own 5-yard line. However, the Tigers quickly moved the ball down the field and took their first lead of the game, as Lawrence found Tee Higgins for a 22-yard touchdown that put the Tigers ahead 14-7.

The Gamecock took their ensuing possession and drove the ball to the Tiger 3-yard line. However they were unable to turn the 73-yard drive into points, as Bentley's passes on third and fourth down fell incomplete and the Tigers took over possession at their own 3-yard line.

The Tigers scored their 21st point of the game, on their longest scoring drive of the year of 97 yards, as the Tigers to their "Fridge" package on fourth-and-goal from the 1-yard line. With defensive linemen Dexter Lawrence and Christian Wilkins in the offense, it was Wilkins who took the toss and dove into the end zone.

Unlike previous seasons, the Gamecocks refused to go away quietly. Facing third-and-4 from their own 33-yard line, Bentley found a wide-open Kiel Pollard for a 67-yard touchdown that cut the Tigers' lead to 21-14.

The Tigers wasted little time pushing the lead back to two scores, as a Lawrence 32-yard scramble and a Choice rush for 24 yards set up Choice's second touchdown of the day and gave the Tigers a momentary 14-point lead because the Gamecocks needed only 1-play, a 75-yard pass from Bentley to Deebo Samuel, to cut the lead back to one score.

Following the first punt of the night by the Tigers, the Gamecocks made their first mistake of the game. Facing third-and-4 from their own 26-yard line, Bentley's pass was intercepted by Tiger linebacker J.D. Davis, his first interception of his career, and the Tigers took over at the Gamecock 33-yard line.

The Tigers were unable to turn the mistake into points, as Justyn Ross dropped a touchdown pass from Lawrence and placekicker Greg Huegel missed his fourth field goal of the season.

On the first possession of the second half, the Tigers rode the coattails of running back Travis Etienne to the end zone. The sophomore amassed 37 of the Tigers 75 yards, including a 2-yard touchdown run that extended the lead to 35-21.

Following only the second punt of the night for the Gamecocks, the Tigers needed only 1:22 and five plays to go 80 yards. Following a Lawrence to Higgins completion for 34 yards to the Gamecock 13-yard line, the Tigers found the end zone on Tavien Feaster's 13-yard touchdown run.

On their next drive, the Gamecocks drove the ball to the Tigers' 2-yard line be- fore, for the second time in the game, they were unable to come away with points, as the Tiger defense held on fourth down.

The Tigers took the ball and marched down the field for their longest touchdown drive of the season, an 11-play, 98-yard drive that culminated in Choice's third rushing touchdown of the game and gave the Tigers a 49-21 lead.

The Gamecocks responded on their next drive, as they found the end zone for the first time in the second half. Bentley orchestrated an eight-play, 75-yard drive that culminated with him finding Samuel for the third time in the game from 32 yards out to cut the lead to 49-28. On the drive, Bentley passed the 400-yard passing mark.

"I thought he played extremely well...gutsy, tough," Gamecock head coach Will Muschamp said."That's who he is. I'm glad he's our quarterback."

Bentley was not finished on the night. Following the second Tiger punt of the night, the Gamecocks needed only four plays to go 74 yards in 1:05—as Bentley found Shi Smith for a 20-yard touchdown.

The Tigers ended the threat, as Etienne found the end zone from 7 yards out that capped off a 54-yard drive with 39 seconds remaining in the game.

"The seniors got their 52nd win. Playing in his last game at Death Valley, Christian Wilkins was amazing," Swinney said. "He had a great touchdown run and got a sack, as well. All in all, we're division champs and state champs, so we're going to enjoy this one tonight. We've got bragging rights for a year, but we'll be ready to move on tomorrow and focus on Pitt."

Tiger Tracks

On Hunter Renfrow's 22-yard catch-and-run, he surpassed 2,000 career receiving yards, becoming just the 13th Tiger in history to hit the milestone.

Travis Etienne went over the 2000-yard career rushing mark in the third quarter of the game.

With his touchdown in the third quarter, Etienne broke the Clemson single-season re- cord for rushing touchdowns with 18.

Clemson set a school-record with 49 rushing touchdowns on the season.

Coaches Corner

Swinney on what is next for the Tigers:

"There's a lot that happened in tonight's game that we can improve on defensively, but the positive is that we won by three touchdowns. But it'll make us better heading into postseason. Now, we'll focus on making more history next week. There's never been a team win four ACC Championship Games in a row, so we're excited about having that opportunity."

THE ACC CHAMPIONSHIP

A week after putting up over 700 yards of offense and 56 points on the South Carolina Gamecocks, the No. 2 Clemson Tigers take their high-flying offense to Charlotte's Bank of America Stadium for a date with the Pittsburgh Panthers in the ACC Championship Game.

But the scary thing for defenses, even after record setting night that saw the Tigers record a school-record three touchdown drives of 95 yards or more,, amass 744 yards their most against South Carolina in series history and marked Clemson's first time posting both 300 passing yards and 300 rushing yards against South Carolina in series history, the Tigers believe they can still be better on offense.

"I think for us, we talked about all the time championship teams play their best ball at the end of the year," co-offensive coordinator Jeff Scott said. "Even though we've done a lot of good things offensively, we've felt like there's another level we can go to. That was really the challenge... Just really focusing in on finishing the regular season.

"There's no doubt we definitely increased and continued the confidence we have as we move forward."

Maybe more surprising than the offenses' outburst against the Gamecocks, was the fact that for the first time all season, it was the defense that had the letdown.

But for Scott, the fact that the offense had to carry the defense Saturday night was only fair.

"The defense, there is no doubt that they helped us out plenty of times," Scott said. "We knew there was going to be opportunities where they were going to lean on us a little bit. What I was proud of, is how the guys responded. I think it's the third time all year where we went in at halftime and were in a tight game and our guys have responded all three times. Being able to go out and get the ball back and go down and score. I'm really proud of that.

"I know the defensive staff is not going to be happy about it, but offensively it was kind of fun to stay in a game where you can run it and throw it for four quarters. If we're up by a lot, then you just kind of slow down your rhythm. It was fun for our offensive guys to go out for four quarters and finish all the way at the end."

The Tigers will now look to turn the page to the Panthers, who rank 71st in scoring defense (27.8 points per game), 80th in rush defense (174.33 yards per game allowed), 61st in pass defense (225.6 yards allowed) and 69th in total defense (allowing 399.9 yards per game).

However, if the Tigers are going to have the same amount of success they had against the Gamecocks, they will need another complete performance from all phases of their offense.

I am really proud of the offensive line—no sacks [allowed] again," Scott said. "I believe we've had one sack [allowed] in [the last] five games, which is incredible. Also, [we] had over 350 yards rushing, which is awesome. Those guys don't get enough credit, since we have a bunch of special, skilled kids around—we've had skilled guys around here for a long time, but now we're running the ball better than we ever have.

"To be a great team you have to be a great defense and a great offense. We knew there would be opportunities when we would have to lean on each other. The best part is how we responded to adversity... We are an offense, defense, special teams."

Tigers ready for challenging Pitt team

While every member of the Clemson senior class undoubtably remembers the last game they played against the Pittsburgh Panthers, their only home loss on a last second kick in 2016, few remember the game as vividly as senior defensive tackle Christian Wilkins.

Wilkins was only a sophomore on the 2016 team, but vividly recalls the game as a wake-up call that eventually propelled the Tigers to the national championship.

"I just remember they just out-executed us," Wilkins said. "They had a good plan for us, a good scheme for us, and they executed it well. Definitely have a lot of respect for them after that game. They were just fearless coming into Death Valley, they just did a good job.

"I feel like then, at that time, 2016, playing against them was a bit of a wake-up call. I feel maybe at that point in the season, things might have been a little relaxed. We might have taken our foot off the throttle a little bit. That was definitely just a wake-up call for us. They really brought it that night."

Even though the Tiger coaching staff preaches that every week is the biggest week of the season, that sense of urgency did not make it to the Tigers in 2016.

And it is that kind of mistake in underestimating an opponent that Wilkins is working hard to not let happen again when they take on the Panthers in the ACC Championship.

"I just know they're going to be ready for this game this coming Saturday. We're going to have to be ready, do a good job of getting prepare," Wilkins said. "Every team, any week, especially in this conference, is capable of beating everyone. It's a tough conference. If you don't bring it, you can definitely get beat.

"Definitely a mindset they're going to bring it this time around, they're going to be ready to play. We have to make sure we execute the game plan and do a good job."

The Panthers will bring the a northern-style of football to the south this weekend, with big offensive linemen, two powerful running backs and a quarterback who can throw the ball and also use his legs as a weapon.

The Tigers had success three weeks ago in taking down a similar style of team, when they traveled to Boston College and defeated the Eagles to clinch the Atlantic Division. But the Tigers understand that the success that they had against one team from above the Mason-Dixon Line does not translate to other teams.

"Pitt definitely presents a big challenge for us," Wilkins said. "Speaking for the defense, what they do on their offense, they have two really good running backs, they have good play-makers, they do a lot of good stuff. We're going to have to bring it, be on our toes, be ready for anything.

"They definitely present a good challenge for us. They're a good team. There's a reason they won their division, because they're obviously very talented and do a good job. We're going to have to be ready for anything they throw at us."

If the Tigers are able to knock off the Panthers for only the second time in school history, it will mean that they accomplished something no team has ever done in the history of the ACC—win fourth straight outright ACC title.

"It's definitely something very special. I mean, it's very hard to accomplish," Wilkins said. "Means a lot to me and my teammates in this program. You don't see this every day, every year, an opportunity for a team to be the so-called top dog in a conference, in a tough conference at that, four years in a row.

"Definitely means a lot to the seniors on the team. We lead the team each and every day. We put it all into the program for four or five years, so it's great to see the results on the field."

Tigers ready for revenge

Senior Clemson wide receiver Hunter Renfrow has been apart of the Tiger football team for what seems like 15 years, which means when the former walk-on speaks people listen—including his teammates.

Having been a part of the winningest class in school and ACC history gives him a great deal of perspective when it comes to the expectations placed on a team like the Tigers.

That perspective came into use this week after a small percentage of the fans were disappointed with the Tigers 56-35 victory over the South Carolina Gamecocks.

"There's criticism everywhere. Even if we beat them 100-3, there's criticism," Renfrow said. 'People are people. They just aren't happy unless it's the best ever. We obviously didn't play as a team up to what we're capable of. But I feel like we haven't done that all year really. Just try to put a consistent effort together. Obviously we do it for the guys in the locker room. There's a lot of outside noise.

We've been through that over the years. We really just try to do it for the guys in the locker room, the coaching staff, just to be able to be accountable to them and try to put our best four quarters on display this Saturday. If it was all easy and we always played our best game every week, there would be no reason to practice. Just show up and play. Sometimes it's good to struggle a little bit."

The struggle paid off for the Tigers the last time they faced their next opponent—the Pittsburgh Panthers, who the Tigers take on Saturday in the ACC Championship at Bank of America Stadium in Charlotte, North Carolina.

The last time the Tigers and the Panthers took the field against each other was in the 2016 season, when the Panthers traveled to Death Valley as 20.5-point underdogs and walked out with a win over the then-second-ranked Tigers.

The Tigers parlayed the loss into a second straight national title later that season. Even without a loss on their record this season, Renfrow believes the Tigers have already had their wake-up call this season, which means the Panthers are getting the full attention of the Tigers this time around.

"For us, I believe it was a lot like the Syracuse game was this year," Renfrow said. "They came into our place and kind of took it to us really. We played well I feel offensively. But it's a team game. They stuck it to us. Kind of like Syracuse this year. Syracuse took it to us. We were just fortunate to win this year.

"I think those two games were similar from that aspect. Coming down the stretch here, we were seeing how their division was shaking up. We were seeing that Pitt might win it. Us seniors especially were looking forward to kind of getting a rematch against them."

The Game

The No. 2 Clemson Tigers (13-0, 9-0 ACC) continued their historical season Saturday night, as they dismantled the Pittsburgh Panthers by a final score of 42-10 in the ACC Championship game at Bank of America Stadium.

With the Tigers victory, they secured their 18th all-time ACC title, became the first ACC team to win four consecutive outright titles, moved to 13-0 for the second time in school history and secured their spot in the College Football Playoff for a fourth straight season.

After an abysmal performance in their last outing against the South Carolina Gamecocks— in which the defense allowed 35 points and more than 500 yards pass- ing—the defense returned to their dominant form, as they allowed only 200 total yards (192 rushing and eight passing).

The ACC Player of the Year wasted little time making his presence felt, as Travis Etienne—who finished with 156 yards on 12 carries and two touchdowns— took a hand- off on the opening play of the game and proceeded to score the fastest touchdown in ACC Championship history. On the play, Etienne needed only 13 seconds to go the 75 yards that gave the Tigers a 7-0 lead.

Following the Tigers' first punt of the game, the Panthers suffered a meltdown. After a punt of 15 yards, the Panthers suffered three penalties that moved the ball from their 39-yard line to their 21-yard line.

On third down, a fumble by quarterback Kenny Pickett was recovered by defensive tackle Christian Wilkins and returned to the 3-yard line. One play later the Tigers found the end zone for the second time, as Etienne capped a one-play drive that extended the lead to 14-0.

The Panthers settled down on their next possession, as they gashed the Tiger defense with their running game. The Panthers attempted only one pass on the drive that ended with a 37-yard field goal that cut the lead to 14-3.

After the Panthers pinned the Tigers on their own 1-yard line, the Panthers forced the Tigers second punt of the game—a 37-yard punt that gave the Panthers the ball on the Tiger 39-yard line. The Panthers needed only six plays, and a 1-yard rush- ing touchdown by Qadree Ollison, to cut the Tigers' lead to 14-10.

The Tigers stopped the bleeding on their ensuing drive, as Etienne scrambled for a 45-yard gain on the first play from scrimmage. Etienne and fellow running back Tavien Feaster carried the ball an additional six times on the drive before quarterback Trevor Lawrence (12-24 for 118 yards and two touchdowns) found Tee Higgins in the end zone for a 5-yard touchdown.

Following a 63-yard punt, the longest in ACC Championship history, by former Calhoun Academy standout Will Spiers, the Panthers drive began at their own 20-yard line.

After two incompletions set up a third-and-10 for the Panthers, Pickett made the first mistake of the night, as his pass was intercepted by A.J. Terrell and returned to the Panther 10-yard line. One-play later, the Tigers extended their lead to 28-10, as Lawrence found Higgins for the second time—their third one-play touchdown drive of the first half.

After both teams exchanged a combined four punts, the Tigers once again found the end zone. After a 21-yard completion to Higgins and an 8-yard run by Lawrence, the Tigers used some trickery, as they called a flea flicker that saw Lawrence find Justyn Ross for a 38-yard gain to the Panther 1-yard line. Senior running back Adam Choice finished off the drive with his first touchdown of the night.

The Tigers added a final score of the night with 3:17 remaining in the game. After Chase Brice entered the game for Lawrence, the Tigers used a 31-yard rush by Choice and a 28-yard rush by Brice to set up a Lyn-J Dixon touchdown that gave the Tigers a 42-10 lead.

Tiger Tracks

Travis Etienne amassed 135 yards, becoming the fifth #Clemson player to rush for over 100 yards in the ACC Championship.

Trevor Lawrence has 15 TD passes and no interceptions in the red zone this year.

Tee Higgins became the Clemson record holder for receiving touchdowns by a sophomore

TIGERS HEAD TO DALLAS

"We're just excited to be the playoffs," Clemson coach Dabo Swinney said. "This is what we worked for all year long. To have an opportunity to get together (today) with all our team and all our families. This is a big deal. We're ready to go to Dallas. I've never been to the Cotton Bowl so I'm really looking forward to it.

This marks the fourth consecutive trip to the playoffs for the Tigers, where they boast a 3-2 overall record— winning two semifinal games and one national title, while losing the 2017 semifinal at the Allstate Sugar Bowl and the 2016 College Football Playoff National Championship Game.

The Cotton Bowl berth brings Clemson's bowl history full circle, The game will be only the Tigers' second all-time appearance in the Cotton Bowl, dating back to the program's first ever bowl bid. That year, Head Coach Jess Neely's Tigers completed a 9-1 campaign in 1939 with a 6-3 victory against Boston College in the 1940 Cotton Bowl.

The victory was a landmark one for Clemson, as in addition to being the program's first bowl game, it represented the school's first win against a Top 20 team.

Clemson won its 53rd game in the last four years Saturday night in the ACC Championship to add to existing school and ACC records for wins held by Clemson's 2018 senior class. It tied the 2014-17 Alabama Crimson Tide for the second-most wins by a senior class in FBS history.

The Tigers will face the Fighting Irish in a bowl game for the first time in school history—having a 2-1 all-time record against the Irish, the last victory coming in 2015.

The Tigers have two common opponents with the Irish this season in the Syracuse Orange and Saturday night's opponent the Pittsburgh Panthers—so, Swinney has already had a chance to see what his Tigers will face in the semifinal game.

"We've had a couple common opponents (with Notre Dame) and gotten a chance to study them a little bit getting ready for Pitt," Swinney said. "What a year Notre Dame has had. I think coach (Brian) Kelly is a coach of the year. It's amazing what they've done with the schedule they've played. To go on the road to some of the venues they've played at. Congratulations to them. We're looking forward to a great matchup."

The winner of the Tigers and Fighting Irish will face the winner of the Capital One Orange Bowl between the No. 1 Alabama Crimson Tide and the No. 4 Oklahoma Sooners in the CFP National Championship in Santa Clara (Jan. 7, 2019).

Swinney dreamed big

"Well, as I've said many times, we're not even close to what I was dreaming about," Swinney said. "I've never been a small dreamer. I had a lot of time as a kid to dream. There wasn't much else left to do.

"I've always dreamed big. The Bible says as a man thinketh, so is he. I've always believed in that. I think you got to be a champion on the inside. You got to believe the right things. You got to be able to see it and have a vision for it. Then you got to go act upon it."

However, the last 10 years have not all been roses for Swinney. In 2010, the Tigers suffered an unexplainable loss in the Meineke Car Care Bowl to South Florida by a final score of 31-26. That game led to the dismissal of Billy Napier as offensive coordinator and the hiring of Chad Morris, now the head coach at Arkansas.

The following season, it was a 70-33 loss to West Virginia in the Orange Bow that led to the dismissal of defensive coordinator Kevin Steele and the hiring of Brent Venables.

But even with two of the worst bowl losses in school history hanging over the program, Swinney continued to believe and dream big.

"You can't be afraid to fail," Swinney said. "Can't let other people put limits on -- let other people put limits on what you can and can't do. Man, absolutely. There's a few things I think we could have done better.

"But absolutely I had a vision for building a program that could be special, that could be hopefully a model in college football. I think we're still under construction, still got a lot of work to do. I continue every day and every year to continue to dream, to believe in a very positive future."

Swinney admitted that he has never been one to settle for a small dream, which seems only fitting for a boy named Dabo from Pelham, Alabama.

"I've never sat around and said, Well, hopefully we can win nine games, this and that," Swinney said. "If we're going to dream, let's extravagantly dream. Let's go all out with it. Let's get a bunch of good people together, be able to sell that and articulate that, get young people to buy into it."

And getting those "young people to buy into" what he was dreaming about at Clemson has become easier and easier with the success the Tigers have had.

Clemson's 2018 senior class improved upon its current winning percentage since 2015 to .930 with their win over the Pittsburgh Panthers Saturday night, which far out- paces the school record set by the 2017 seniors (. 877, 50-7). The class can now finish with a winning percentage of no worse than .914, which makes the 2018 senior class the first in school history to field a winning percentage of .900 or better.

Clemson also won its 53rd game in the last four years to add to existing school and ACC records for wins held by Clemson's 2018 senior class. It tied the 2014-17

Alabama Crimson Tide for the second-most wins by a senior class in FBS history.

"Man, it's amazing what you can do when you get a bunch of people to come together for a common purpose, singleness of purpose, one heartbeat. It's powerful," Swinney said. "It's powerful. It's what the Bible says. Two can accomplish more than, twice as much as one. Great synergy when you got a lot of people that believe in that same vision. That's what we got at Clemson."

Swinney and Kelly excited about trip to Dallas

"Well, just, first of all, that stadium. What a great venue. I've never been there," Clemson head coach Dabo Swinney said. "I've obviously seen it on TV. So I'm looking forward to playing a game in such an incredible environment and spending some extended time in Dallas"

While Swinney may be excited to go and see AT&T Stadium, the $1.15-billion dollar home to the Dallas Cowboys, the Fighting Irish have played in the stadium in the past.

But even though they have already played inside the stadium affectionately known as "Jerry's World," for owner Jerry Jones, there is still the awe of playing in such a big stadium on such a big stage and seeing yourself on such a big video board.

"We played there a few years back, one of our Shamrock Series games against Arizona State, and you just got to catch yourself from looking up at the scoreboard all the time," Notre Dane head coach Brian Kelly said. "It's just a great environment."

Unlike some head coaches whose only focus is winning the game, both Swinney and Kelly are looking forward to the experience that traveling to Dallas with their respective teams will bring.

"Look, what happens when you're involved in this, you get another chance to be with your guys. I mean, that's why we coach," Kelly said. "We do more than just stand on the sideline. It's an investment that we have with our team and the relationships that we build with our guys that we get one more chance to be with them.

"So just getting that opportunity to prepare and see them through their process for hopefully a couple more games, and then to be in a great venue like AT&T Stadium. It's a great environment.The always effervescent Swinney is also looking forward to one last trip with a group of seniors that have already written themselves into the history books with a list of records that will be difficult to surpass.

"When I've been to Dallas, it's been kind of in and out," Swinney said. "But just all the things I've heard about the Cotton Bowl in general, the hospitality and the wonderful committee folks that they have there.

"But just having a chance to compete against a great team and again on a great stage and representing Clemson the very best we can. That's what I'm looking forward to, and seeing our players just continue to enjoy their journey."

THE GAME:

ARLINGTON, Texas— The No. 2 Clemson Tigers (14-0) are headed to Santa Clara for the 2019 College Football Playoff National Championship (Jan. 7, 8 p.m., ESPN) after they handled the No. 3 Notre Dame Fighting Irish (12-1) in the CFP semifinal at the Goodyear Cotton Bowl Saturday by a final score of 30-3

"I'm just thankful that we got the opportunity to be up here (on stage) because that means that we won the game," Clemson head coach Dabo Swinney said. 'We achieved our goal. I'm really proud of our team and our staff. Just an amazing performance. A dominant performance. Obviously, had some adversity. But these guys stepped up and did an awesome job."

Anyone who was waiting on true freshman quarterback Trevor Lawrence to have a "freshman moment" was left waiting, as he played one of the best games of his career. Lawrence completed 27 of 39 passes for 327 yards, three touchdowns and no interceptions in a performance that earned him MVP honors for the game.

"I definitely envisioned him being a great player," Swinney said. "There's no question about that. That's why we recruited him. I saw that back in the spring. And after four games I felt like he deserved to go start. And he gave us the best chance to win and play at an explosive level. He had great understanding and command of what we were doing.

"So my vision was for him to lead us that next week. And then, when things changed, well, okay, well now we'll see what he does for the rest of the year. And he just has done an incredible job."

After both teams exchanged punts on their opening possession, Clemson defensive end Clelin Ferrell forced a fumble of quarterback Ian Book on the Irish's second drive of the game that gave the Tigers the ball their own 47-yard line.

The Tigers opened the scoring after Book's fumble, as quarterback Trevor Lawrence led the Tigers to the Fighting Irish 22-yard line where the Tigers settled for a 40-yard field goal by Greg Huegel gave the Tigers a 3-0 lead.

The Fighting Irish answered the Tigers on their next drive. A pass from Book to running back Dexter Williams for 16 yards and a pass interference penalty on Clemson aided a 66-yard drive that resulted in a 28-yard field goal by Justin Yoon and tied the game 3-3.

After both teams exchanged punts, the Tigers found the end zone. Following a 7-yard run by Adam Choice and a 6-yard pass from Lawrence to Trevion Thompson, the Tigers went for the home run when Lawrence found Justyn Ross for a 52-yard touchdown pass. The ensuing extra-point was blocked by the Fighting Irish.

After a second forced punt of the game, the Tigers took over at their own 15-yard line and needed only eight plays to add to their lead. Facing a fourth-and-14, Lawrence founds Ross for a 42-yard touchdown that capped an 85-yard drive and gave the Tigers a 16-3 lead.After a 59-yard punt by the Fighting Irish gave the Tigers the ball on their own 20-yard line with 48 seconds remaining, the Tigers needed only 46 to add to their lead.

"That touchdown drive with 48 seconds and one timeout was a huge, huge momentum boost for our team," Swinney said.

After Lawrence found a wide-open Hunter Renfrow for a 32-yard gain, a 15-yard roughing the passer penalty moved the ball to the Fighting Irish 19-yard line with 9 seconds remaining in the first half. Lawrence needed only seven to find Tee Higgins in the end zone, who made an acrobatic one-handed catch, that gave the Tigers a 23-3 lead.

After the teams exchanged a combined three punts to start the second half, the Tigers got the spark they were looking for after safety Nolan Turner intercepted Book's pass and returned it to the Tiger 29-yard line.

"Nolan Turner's play was huge," Swinney said. "Brent [Venables] and our staff, they do an amazing job. And our secondary. Everybody -- our secondary has been reading for three weeks how terrible they are. I mean, Good Lord, we have one sub-par game that you win by three touchdowns and all of a sudden our secondary is terrible. I thought they were ready."

Following the change of possession, the Tigers turned to running back Travis Etienne—who, after two plays, took the third play to the end zone on a 62-yard run that gave the Tigers a 30-3 lead.

"You keep giving that ball to Number 9, [Travis Etienne] if you give him 15 touches or more, something good is going to happen. And simple as that," Swinney said. "He was close on a couple of them where the safety was the unblocked guy that got him down. But on that third one there, man, he just popped it. He was gone. But that's what he can do. That's why you just make sure he gets enough touches. You don't give up on it. You stay patient."

The National Championship

The R.O.Y. bus may have made it's final stop, as the No. 2 Clemson Tigers are set to take on the No.1 Alabama Crimson Tide in the College Football Playoff National Championship Jan. 7 (8 p.m., ESPN) at Levi's Stadium in Santa Clara, California.

The R.O.Y. bus, or "rest of y'all" bus, was the one that Tiger head coach Dabo Swinney claimed that the Tigers, and the rest of the college football world, were on this season, as it appeared to be the Crimson Tide and everyone else. But Monday, Swinney changed his tune.

"You know, I think that this is clearly the two best teams in Alabama and Clemson, and it's going to be an exciting game," Swinney said. "I mean, this is the way it should be, and we know we've got a huge challenge. Want to congratulate Alabama, as well, for just another amazing year, and Coach (Nick) Saban and what he's done, it's just – they're hard to beat.

"But we're excited about the challenge, and we're off and running with our prep, and got a short week to kind of get ready to make the long flight out there on Friday. But we're so thankful to have the opportunity to be a part of it."

After spending the majority of the season preaching the gap between the Crimson Tide and the rest of college football, Swinney finally admitted that his Tigers are, at least, on par with the Crimson Tide.

"I mean, these are two really good teams that are both hard to beat, and you've got to do the little things to give yourself a chance, whether it be that field position battle, it's where your guys are, it's your footwork, positioning, it's technique, because you just don't have a lot of room for error, either team," Swinney said. "I think when you look at this game, I think both teams are kind of mirror images of each other to be honest with you, really good defenses, dynamic quarterbacks, very talented running backs, and explosive skill, and just kind of built in the trenches. We're so similar."

With this year's being the fourth meeting between these two teams in the last four years, many in the media are already drawing the comparisons to the Rocky movies.

But for Swinney, the thing that a fourth meeting means to his Tigers is simply they know what to expect when they line up against the Crimson Tide.

"We've played them now four years in a row, and this is a veteran team that we have," They understand that this is a game where you just have so little margin for error. I mean, it's two or three plays, literally. You've got to have great preparation mentally and physically to get yourself ready."

While Swinney is worried about getting prepared for a team that mirrors his in so many ways, Saban is worried about preparing for one of the most dynamic offense and defenses that his Crimson Tide team have faced this season.

"Coach Swinney and his team have had an outstanding year, and being 14-0 and ACC champs, they've got a really nice group of players on both sides of the ball," Saban said. "They're a complete team in terms of their offense being very productive, averaging 44 points a game and 530 yards. The freshman quarterback, Trevor Lawrence, has done a fantastic job for them all year long. They've got great balance on offense in terms of their ability to run and throw and a talented group of receivers.

"Their defense is one of the best defensive teams in the country in lots of different categories, and they've got a really good front seven, and they're very well-coached. This is certainly a complete team."

Whether or not people want to use the Rocky storylines for the fourth iteration of the Clemson-Alabama game, if the Tigers are going to be considered a rival for the Crimson Tide they need to find a way to beat them.

"Somebody asked me the other day if they are becoming our rival and I'm like, 'Well, you gotta win a few times before it can really become a rivalry I think,'" Swinney said. "They have been unbelievably dominant. It's incredible what they have done the last 10 years and the championships they have won. They're a tough out for anybody."

Mission almost accomplished

The Clemson Tiger are four quarters away from what they set out to do—win a national championship.

It was 368 days ago that the Tigers had their season end at the hands of the Alabama Crimson Tide, 24-6, in the College Football Playoff semifinal at the Allstate Sugar Bowl. It was that loss that prompted the return of the entire defensive line and offensive lineman Mitch Hyatt —all of whom said they had "unfinished business."

Now, after 368 days the Tigers, as fate would have it, will get their chance at redemption—against the Crimson Tide nonetheless.

"It is definitely special. All the work we put in, the leadership by the seniors and the vets on the team, the coaches, the staff," defensive tackle Christian Wilkins said. "We put in so much work each and every day it is just special to be here. I've experienced a lot of success in my time here but it really never gets old. The challenge of trying to get back here every year is the most fun part.

"You face different adversities, you go up against different challenges, and each year is different and it is special each and every time because we try and find ways to get better, to challenge ourselves and to challenge our teammates. This is just another opportunity to compete in the National Championship and I am looking forward to next week."

The Tigers may be looking forward to next weeks' game against the Crimson Tide in the national championship, but make no mistake about their intentions—they are not going to Santa Clara for the sun or sand.

They are going there with one goal in mind—bringing home the school's third national title.

"Next week is all business," defensive tackle and former Orangeburg-Wilkinson standout Albert Huggins said. "This week was fun and all, but next week is a business trip—that is all. Next week is about finishing the season the way that we wanted to all along—winning the national championship. So, that is our goal."

The Tigers have accomplished every goal on their season checklist—"win the opener", "win the division", "win the state championship" and "win the ACC"—the only one left is to "win the closer."

"We know what is on the line this week," Huggins said. "We have a chance to end the season with a win and take care of our final goal. The time for playing is over, this trip is all about business."

The Tigers' trip to Santa Clara will not be the week-long, fun-filled adventure they experienced in Dallas. Instead, it will be a business trip.

The Tigers will fly to California Friday, have the media day Saturday, Sunday the two head coaches will have their final press conference and Monday (8 p.m., ESPN) the Tigers will take on the Crimson Tide in the CFP National Championship at Levi's Stadium.

"Really proud of my guys," head coach Dabo Swinney said. "They've worked their tails off all year to put themselves in this situation, so we're excited about heading out to California later in the week.

"But we're excited about the challenge, and we're off and running with our prep, and got a short week to kind of get ready to make the long flight out there on Friday.

But we're so thankful to have the opportunity to be a part of it."

SANTA CLARA, Calif.— The No. 2 Clemson Tigers captured their third football national championship in school history Monday night when they demolished the No.1 Alabama Crimson Tide in the College Football Playoff National Championship by a final score of 44-16 at Levi's Stadium.

"We bent a little, but we never broke. We punched back. This group had the eye of the Tiger tonight," Clemson head coach Dabo Swinney said. "And listen, Alabama, this is the most amazing champion ever, the University of Alabama and what they've done with Coach Saban. And for our guys to come out here tonight and perform like they did—It's just our staff.

"We had an amazing plan, we had a great week, and I felt like we had the better team. I felt like if we could get a couple of breaks, we could pull away, and the couple of turnovers and the big plays... I said coming in yesterday that big plays and turnovers -- you win those two things, you win 98 percent of the time, and we won it in a big way tonight."

With the victory, the Tigers became the second team to win multiple national championships in the CFP era (2014), became the first major college team in the modern era to go 15-0 and broke the school record for wins in a season (previously 14 games in 2015 and 2016).

"There's never been a 15-0 team, and I know we're not supposed to be here -- we're just little ole Clemson, and I'm not supposed to be here -- but we are and I am, and how bout them Tigers, man," Swinney said. "I'm so proud of our guys, these seniors. We beat Notre Dame and Alabama, we left no doubt, and we walk off this field tonight as the first 15-0 team in college football history.

"All the credit, all the glory goes to the good Lord, number one, and number two to these young people. When you get a young group of people that believe, are passionate, they love each other, they sacrifice, they're committed to a purpose, you better look out. Great things can happen, and that's what you saw tonight."

After the Tigers went three-and-out on their opening possession, it was the defense that provided the first score. Facing a second-and-2 from their own 28-yard line, Crimson Tide quarterback Tua Tagovailoa's pass was intercepted by A.J. Terrell, who returned the interception 44 yards for a touchdown.

The Crimson Tide responded on their next drive, as Tagovailoa found a wide-open Jerry Jeudy for a 62-yard touchdown that capped a three-play, 75-yard drive that tied the game 7-7.

On the Tigers' ensuing possession, the Tigers faced a third-and-14 at their own 21-yard line when quarterback Trevor Lawrence (20-32 for 347 yards and three touchdowns) found Tee Higgins for a 62-yard gain to the Crimson Tide 17-yard line. Travis Etienne finished the drive off with a 17-yard touchdown run that gave the Tigers the lead 14-7.

Tagovailoa led the Crimson Tide down the field once again, and once again the Crimson Tide capitalized when Tagovailoa found Hale Hentges for a one-yard touchdown that brought the Crimson Tide within one-point after the extra point was missed by Joseph Bulovas.

Following the Tigers second punt of the game, the Crimson Tide took over at their own 48-yard line. The Crimson Tide drove the ball to the Tigers' 3-yard line before a false start and a pass for a loss of 4 yards forced the Crimson Tide to settle for a 25-yard field goal. The field goal gave the Crimson Tide their first lead of the game.

Following a free-kick out of bounds and a pass interference penalty, the Tigers took over at their own 50-yard line and needed only six plays to retake the lead.

After the penalty, Lawrence found Tavien Feaster for a 26-yard pass, and following two runs that netted 5 yards, found Higgins for a 14-yard reception that moved the ball to the Crimson Tide 5-yard line. Two plays later, Etienne found the end zone for the second time in the game and gave the Tigers a 21-16 lead.

The Crimson Tide gave the ball right back to the Tigers, as Tagovailoa threw his second interception of the game—this one intercepted by Trayvon Mullen—that was returned to the Crimson Tide 47-yard line.

The Tigers wasted little time making the Crimson Tide pay for the turnover, as Lawrence led the Tigers on an eight-play, 47-yard touchdown drive—capped off by a 5-

yard touchdown pass from Lawrence to Etienne that extended the lead to 28-16.

Following the Crimson Tide's first punt of the game, the Tigers extended their lead—as they needed only eight plays to set up a 36-yard field goal by Greg Huegel that gave the Tigers a 31-16 lead.

The Crimson Tide opened the second half with the ball and moved to the Clemson 24-yard line before they lined up for a 40-yard field goal attempt on fourth-and-6. Instead of kicking the field goal, the Crimson Tide attempted a fake field goal that was snuffed out by Nyles Pinckney for a loss of 2 yards.

The Tigers needed only three plays to go the 76 yards and extend their lead to 37-16, as Lawrence found a wide-open Justyn Ross for a 74-yard touchdown on third-and-8.

"It's amazing," Lawrence said. "I get a lot of credit for stuff that I'm not even half of it. My teammates, these coaches did an unbelievable job, and I just love everyone that's been a part of this journey. It's been an awesome journey and it's really unbelievable."

The Tigers continued adding to their lead, following a failed fourth down attempt at the Clemson 14-yard line. Lawrence found Higgins for a 5-yard touchdown that capped off a 12-play, 89-yard drive and extended the lead to 44-16.

On their ensuing possession, the Crimson Tide put together their best drive of the second half. However, their 66-yard drive ended at the Clemson 7-yard line, as Tigers stopped Tagovailoa for a 7 yard loss on fourth-and-2.

Tiger Tracks:

The 31 points in the first half by Clemson is a postseason school record. Previous best 27 versus

Oklahoma in first half of 2014 Champs Sports Bowl and 1986 Gator vs Stanford.

With his first PAT, his 72nd of the season, kicker Greg Huegel broke his own single-season team record of 71 PATs from 2016. Huegel has accounted for three of the top five seasons in PATs in school history.

During the first half, Clemson (651) became the second team in ACC history to score 650 points in a single season (Florida State, 723 in 2013).

Clemson's 31 first-half points represented the first time Alabama had allowed 31 points in a single half since the 2014 Sugar Bowl.

Tigers are still members of the ROY Bus, at least according to Swinney:

"We drove the ROY bus all the way out here to wherever the heck in California we are to play a football game in a beautiful stadium and a beautiful place," Swinney said.

"We're proud members of the ROY bus, so for all them other teams out there on that bus, hey listen, I hope that you get a little hope from us and a little inspiration that if we can do it, anybody can do it."

Notes:

<u>WITH THE WIN...</u>

- Clemson won its third football national championship in school history, joining the 1981 and 2016 squads. It marks the sixth national championship in any sport in Clemson history (1981 football, 1984 men's soccer, 1987 men's soccer, 2003 men's golf, 2016 football, 2018 football).
- Clemson joined Florida State (three) as the only schools to win three national titles as members of the ACC. Pitt (nine), Miami (five), Georgia Tech (four) have also won at least three national championships, but all of Pitt and Miami's titles predated the schools joining the ACC, as did three of Georgia Tech's four titles.
- Clemson became the second team to win multiple national championships in the College Football Playoff era since 2014 (Alabama).
- Clemson became the first major college football team in the modern era to go 15-0. No major college football team had won 15 games since the 19th century, when Penn posted a 15-0 mark in 1897.
- The 2018 Tigers broke the school record of 14 wins, a mark previously shared with the 2015 and 2016 Tigers.
- Clemson finished its sixth undefeated season (1900, 1906, 1948, 1950, 1981, 2018) and fourth perfect season (1900, 1948, 1981, 2018) in school history.
- When the final AP poll is released, Clemson will become the first team since its own 2016 squad to finish the

season as the AP No. 1 despite never appearing at No. 1 at any point of the season. The 2018 Tigers were the 20th team in AP Poll history to do so (2018 Clemson, 2016 Clemson, 2015 Alabama, 2014 Ohio State, 2011 Alabama, 2006 Florida, 2005 Texas, 2002 Ohio State, 1992 Alabama, 1989 Miami, 1987 Miami, 1986 Penn State, 1983 Miami, 1982 Penn State, 1977 Notre Dame, 1973 Notre Dame, 1970 Nebraska, 1965 Alabama, 1964 Alabama and 1946 Notre Dame).

- By virtue of No. 2 Clemson beating No. 1 Alabama, lower-ranked seeds improved to 5-0 all-time in the College Football Playoff National Championship, including victories by No. 4 Ohio State (vs. No. 2 Oregon) in 2014, No. 2 Alabama (vs. No. 1 Clemson) in 2015, No. 2 Clemson (vs. No. 1 Alabama) in 2016 and No. 4 Alabama (vs. No. 3 Georgia) in 2017.
- Clemson improved to 5-2 all-time in College Football Playoff contests and pushed its record in CFP National Championships to 2-1.
- Clemson's seniors improved to 55-4 since 2015 to give the senior class a .932 career winning percentage, breaking the school record set by the 2017 seniors (.877, 50-7). The 2018 senior class became the first in school history to field a winning percentage of .900 or better.
- Clemson won its 15th straight game, tying a 15-game streak from 1947-49 for the second-longest winning streak in program history. It is now the longest active FBS winning streak in the country.
- Clemson earned its 103rd win of the decade. Clemson, Alabama and Ohio State are the only FBS schools to win 100 games in the 2010s.
- Clemson improved its all-time bowl record to 24-20 and its all-time postseason record, including conference championship games, to 29-21.
- The additional bowl win gave the Tigers victories in eight of their last 10 bowl games since the 2012 season. One of

the two losses came during the 2015 season in a National Championship that was preceded by an Orange Bowl win, so Clemson has won a bowl game in eight of the last nine years.

- Clemson improved to 2-5 all-time against AP No. 1-ranked teams, with both wins coming against Alabama in College Football Playoff National Championships.
- Clemson improved to 18-2 against AP Top 25 teams since 2015. Clemson's 18 wins against Top 25 teams are the second-most in the country in that span.
- The 2018 season will mark Clemson's eighth straight year meeting or exceeding its preseason rankings in the AP and USA Today polls. Clemson has now exceeded its preseason ranking each of the last eight years in the coaches poll and has exceeded its preseason ranking in the AP poll seven of the last eight (Clemson was picked No. 8 in the 2013 AP preseason poll in 2013 and finished No. 8).
- Clemson evened its all-time record in the month of January at 11-11.
- Clemson won its 30th consecutive outdoor game. Clemson is now 55-1 in its last 56 outdoor games dating back to the middle of the 2014 campaign.
- Clemson became just third school to win a National Championship and the AFCA Academic Achievement Award in same year, joining 1988 Notre Dame and 2017 Alabama.
- Head coach Dabo Swinney became only the second active FBS coach to win multiple national championships, joining Alabama's Nick Saban (six, including one at LSU).
- Swinney improved to 14-6 in postseason play, including both conference championships and bowl games.
- Swinney earned his ninth bowl victory all-time, extending his existing school record over Danny Ford (six). The

ninth bowl victory pulled him within two of Bobby Bowden's conference record (11).

- Swinney's earned his eighth bowl victory since 2012 against coaches with national championships to their credit at various NCAA levels (two each against Urban Meyer, Bob Stoops and Nick Saban, one each against Brian Kelly and Les Miles).
- Swinney earned his 116th career victory to push his career record to 116-30. His 116th career win tied him with College Football Hall of Fame coaches Fritz Crisler and Mike Bellotti in coaching wins at the Division I level.

Made in the USA
Lexington, KY
15 January 2019